Down the Crooked Road

My Autobiography

Mary Black

TRANSWORLD IRELAND

TRANSWORLD IRELAND
an imprint of The Random House Group Limited
20 Vauxhall Bridge Road, London SW1V 2SA
www.transworldbooks.co.uk

Transworld Ireland is part of the Penguin Random House group of companies
whose addresses can be found at global.penguinrandomhouse.com

Penguin
Random House
UK

First published in 2014 by Transworld Ireland
an imprint of Transworld Publishers
Transworld Ireland paperback edition published 2015

A CIP catalogue record for this book
is available from the British Library.

ISBN
9781848271883

Typeset in 12/16pt Berkeley Old Style by Falcon Oast Graphic Art Ltd.
Printed and bound by CPI Group (UK) Ltd, Croydon, CR0 4YY.

Penguin Random House is committed to a sustainable
future for our business, our readers and our planet. This book is made
from Forest Stewardship Council® certified paper.

MIX
Paper from
responsible sources
FSC® C016897

1 3 5 7 9 10 8 6 4 2

MARY BLACK was born into a musical family in Dublin. She was one of five children and began singing with her siblings at a very early age. Over the course of her long career she has become one of Ireland's best-loved artists and has achieved international acclaim across Europe, Australia, Japan and the USA. She has shared stages, television studios and recording studios with some of the most acclaimed performers of our day – from Van Morrison and Joan Baez to Emmylou Harris and Imelda May – and has recorded numerous multi-platinum albums. Her latest album, *Stories from the Steeple*, was released in 2011.

Mary has won countless awards during the course of her career, including the Irish Recorded Music's Best Female Artist Award (six times) and the *Irish Post*'s Lifetime Achievement Award in 2006. She has three children and two granddaughters, and lives in Dublin with her husband Joe. Visit her website at www.mary-black.net

www.transworldbooks.co.uk

www.transworldireland.ie

For Bonnie and Fía

Prologue

Me, facing me . . .

I HARDLY RECOGNIZE the person sitting across from me. I have known her all my life but she looks almost like a stranger now. Her jet-black hair has been swept back into a bouffant, her make-up has been applied professionally, with red lips and long dark lashes around her green eyes. It is the first time I've been alone all day. In ten minutes I will be standing on stage performing to a sell-out crowd at the Royal Albert Hall. As I stare at myself in the mirror, the heat from the halogen bulbs adds to the panic rising in my stomach. 'How did I get myself into this?'

It's a stupid question really, but one I ask myself often; like a mantra of disbelief I whisper these words before I go on stage. In truth I have been preparing for this very moment for many days and know exactly how I have gotten myself into it. I had recently signed a record deal with Grapevine Records in England, who were going to film the gig to bring out on video. Though I hated the idea, they insisted that I go shopping with a stylist for the concert. He took me to places like Harrods, Selfridges and Harvey Nichols, places that seemed over-priced and decadent to me. It was a complete disaster. I hated everything he suggested. In the end, and to the dismay of the stylist and the record company, I wore something of my own: a long black jacket with gold buttons (fitted with my signature shoulder pads) and a short skirt with black tights (all bought from Penney's in Dublin). My hair had just been done by Anthony and my make-up by Annie, both of whom had been specially flown over from Ireland. They had worked with me on previous occasions and knew what I liked. I didn't usually get this kind of treatment, but tonight was special, I needed to look my best.

Moments ago the room had been buzzing with the comings and goings of hairdressers, make-up artists, photographers, representatives from the record company as well as family and well-wishers from the venue. And now, even though I sit alone, the room around me seems to buzz with the silence of their absence and the anticipation of the momentous task that lies ahead. I begin to realize this moment is the culmination of years and years of work, and I have been waiting for it my whole life. I find myself thinking back to how this began all those years ago in a tiny, cramped bedroom in Dublin. Just me, my brother and a battered, second-hand tape recorder.

* * *

'But why, Seamus? Betty Day brought out her skippin'
rope and all the girls are playin'. Why can't you do it
yourself?'

I'm eleven years old and I'm standing impatiently in
the doorway of my bedroom. Its faded green wallpaper is
crumbling at the high corners of the ceiling. Two steel-
frame beds take up the majority of the small room, which
is shared by my three brothers, Seamus (Shay), Michael
and Martin. A statue of Our Lady and a picture of the
Sacred Heart watch over us from above the fireplace. I
glimpse Our Lady from the corner of my eye, blue veiled,
hands joined in prayer. I grimace slightly as I see the
crack in her forehead, an injury sustained during one of
our games, something I always felt a Catholic guilt over.

Sixteen-year-old Shay is sitting in front of the fire-
place, his old reel-to-reel tape recorder, which he had
bought second-hand from 'Maurice For Bargains' on
Kelly's Corner, placed carefully on the woodworm-
riddled chest of drawers. He is asking me to sing a new
song for him, one he had just heard on BBC Radio
Scotland. His pride and joy, an Egmond guitar bought for
£12 with his confirmation money, is cradled in his arms.

At the time I thought this purchase was a bit of a
waste of money. Our father was a musician and the house
was packed full of musical instruments. We had a fiddle
(which, in a few years, Martin, then aged eight, would

make his instrument), a mandolin, a banjo (all of which my father played, although my brother Michael, who was around thirteen at the time, started to pick up the mandolin and the banjo, too); a button accordion; a few tin whistles; a big old upright piano, even a set of bagpipes that resided under my father's bed and never got played. To me it seemed we had almost every instrument there was to be had but all Shay saw was the absence of a guitar.

Shay looks away as if annoyed at my question. It is one I know the answer to already but I don't quite understand why. As a child Shay was extremely musical, he had a beautiful singing voice, but his voice had begun to crack and squeak between high and low registers when he spoke.

'Ah come on, I have a lovely new song I want you to learn.'

Though I could hear the laughter of my friends down on the street below there was something in that room that called to me. There were times when we squabbled; Shay would tease me and drive me up the walls, like most big brothers do to their sisters. But music and singing was the one thing we could do together without killing each other. I let out a long exaggerated sigh and stomped dramatically into the room, plonking myself down on one of the beds. 'Fine!' I say as I cross my arms and stare out the window, determined to pretend this is a huge chore for me.

A flicker of a smile reaches the corners of my brother's light blue eyes, but he hides it quickly. Talented and intelligent, Shay was the apple of my mother's eye. She was over the moon when he earned a scholarship to Synge Street Secondary School.

In case I make a bolt for the door, Shay gets to the point fast and turns to the reel-to-reel tape recorder. 'Right, so this is it. It's a song called "Schooldays Over".' He hits the play button and I watch as the two large spools begin to spin and the room is filled with a soft crackling buzz. A slow melodic guitar begins and then the low folk voice of Ewan MacColl fills the room.

Schooldays over, come on then John,
Time to be getting your pit boots on,
On with your sack and your moleskin trousers
Time you were on your way,
Time you were learning the pitman's job and earning a
*   pitman's pay.*

I lean forward and listen intently, instantly forgetting about my previously staged huff. The verse starts low and sweet but I can hear a sadness behind the words. As we listen Shay tells me the song is about a mother calling her son to get up and go down to work in the mines for the first time, even though he's only a boy. I understood then why I felt sad listening to it.

11

The song ends and the room goes silent and I think to myself, it's such a sad song. Shay hands me the lyrics, which he has already written down from the recording, and we start. We play it over and over, Shay playing his guitar and correcting my mistakes. As we listen again and again to Ewan's voice, making sure we have it right, I do not notice the lengthening shadows from the window moving across the floor.

Our mother's voice finally breaks us out of our concentration. Calling from the hall two floors below she's shouting up to us, 'Seamus! Mary! Your tea is ready!' Hours had passed. My mother's voice annoys me; it is as if she has broken a spell. My brow furrows and my shoulders relax in defeat as an unexpected feeling of disappointment comes over me at the thought of having to leave the room. I peek at Shay, realizing that my faked lack of interest must be very obvious to him right now, but I also see that he is just as annoyed as me at the interruption.

I jump up off the bed, a little stiff from the hours of sitting in the same position, and stretch my arms in the air as I walk towards the door. I catch sight of myself in the old full-length mirror on the front of the wardrobe. I'm small for my age, with shoulder-length curly black hair and a fringe; I'm wearing an old lemon-coloured dress that shows up how dark my skin is from playing outside all summer. I can't help but notice the look of satisfaction on my face as I walk by the mirror and it stops me in my tracks. There's something else in my expression, too, that I can't quite put my finger on. Those few hours had sparked something in me; this song was a new departure for me but I knew I was making good progress with it, getting to the heart of it. It was a feeling I'd never really experienced before, and I was eager to feel it again. I turn back to Shay, who's putting away his guitar. 'So, when are we going to finish it?'

Two sharp knocks on the dressing-room door bring me back to the moment, and the halogen-rimmed mirror in front of me. A man's voice with a familiar Northern accent is talking to me through the door. 'Are ye ready, Mary?' With those four words the brief peacefulness of my memories fades quickly and my nerves come rushing back.

'Yeah, one second, Damian!' I answer hastily as I check myself one last time in the mirror. I take a deep breath and walk to the door. Damian, my tour manager of five years, stands at the ready outside. 'All right?' he asks with a smile.

'I'm as right as I'll ever be!' I answer as usual.

Within moments we are standing behind the stage and Damian is giving the signal for the band to start. I hear Noel on drums count four beats and the band begin, Carl playing that familiar melodic line of 'Another Day' on his sax. For a second I think again of that little girl who couldn't wait to get back to that room to sing. The crowd erupts as I walk on stage, tambourine in hand . . .

> Hey little brother, the winds of the world
> Have ruffled your soft and weakened wings.
> And though I can't hold you, as I look into your eyes,
> I can see the film that disappointment brings.

1

'Down Our Street'

I WOKE EARLY that morning, full of excitement. Everybody in the house was still asleep, including my three brothers. Ours was a simple bedroom with two beds, one I shared with my little brother Martin and one shared by my older brothers Shay and Michael. The only other furniture was a big old rickety wardrobe beside the door. My eyes shot to that wardrobe the second I woke up because hanging from it was my brand new school uniform. It had been there, waiting for the big day, for the last week. To me, it seemed as anxious to be worn as I was to wear it. Every morning since my mother had hung it there I would wake and my eyes would jump towards it, examining the crisp white shirt, the fresh new gymslip and the royal blue cardigan, longing for it to be the morning when I could finally wear them. It hadn't been hugely expensive to buy but it was more than my parents could afford. I knew that because Mammy told me to thank my auntie Frances the next time I saw her.

Frances was my mother's older sister and she often helped my parents out when they needed it. She used to buy all five of us our Christmas shoes and Easter sandals every year, and she was always very good to us.

The night before, in preparation for the special occasion, I had been scrubbed to within an inch of my life in the old tin bath in front of the fire. But now, the big day had finally arrived.

As I lay there wide awake, staring at the most beautiful outfit I had ever called my own, I heard the familiar sound of the train pulling off from Harcourt Street on its way to Bray. I jumped out of bed and ran to the window. I waved frantically at the passengers, as I did most mornings until I saw them wave back and the train pulled out of view. From the window I could see our and all the neighbours' back gardens, bare and weed-ridden with washing lines hanging in most; broken-down walls separated them, walls that once might have been grand and strong when the wealthy lived here. At the end of the gardens was the back of an old factory, past which I had never ventured, as I was only four and a half. It was 1959 and this was to be my first day of school.

I was born on the twenty-third of May 1955 in Holles Street Hospital in Dublin. I spent the next twenty-four years living with my family at 69 Charlemont Street. It was originally a street full of beautiful Georgian houses but, like many streets in Dublin, by the time I was born it had deteriorated into open-door tenement houses. Four or five families would live in one house, averaging two or three rooms per family. Our house was one of the few on the street that had a closed door; in other words, you had a key to get in. Mammy and Daddy moved into one room at number 69 after they got married in the late 1940s. By the time I came along they managed to get two more rooms in the house, which we used as bedrooms. Most of the old tenement houses had no bathroom or toilet, or even running water. Usually, the toilet was out the back. There would be an all-purpose tap in the back garden that was used for domestic and personal washing and cleaning. Because Daddy was in the building trade he got together with some of his friends and built an indoor toilet in our house – it was the height of luxury on our street.

We lived comfortably enough in Charlemont Street. All the kids slept in one bedroom and my parents in the other, until my mother got pregnant for the fifth time. When Mammy went into hospital to have Frances, my brothers and me moved out of our home for about a week. Daddy had to work, so he wasn't there to take care of us when we got home from school. As well as that, there seemed to be a general consensus that men didn't know how to take care of children and in such circumstances they would be left with female relatives or neighbours. In our case it was our granny and Auntie Frances who lived on Cork Street nearby. We didn't mind the change; all us kids loved Mammy's mother and sister.

There was great excitement at the time because we knew there might be a new baby coming but didn't know what it was going to be. Back then I didn't know where babies came from. We were told Mammy was going into hospital for something and might come back with a baby. There were no cabbage patch stories for us. We knew that babies came from the hospital, but believed, as our mother told us, that the nurses came around the wards with a basket of babies and all the women in the ward got to pick one.

As an only girl with three brothers I hoped, and probably prayed to God, for my mammy to pick a little sister for me. But I knew that might not happen because, as my mother also told me, you can't tell if the babies are boys or girls when you look at them in the basket.

Soon we got the news that Mammy had picked the only girl in the basket and she was going to be named Frances. I remember the day my little sister was brought home from hospital. I was out playing on the road in Eugene Street when Auntie Frances called me from the door with this little bundle in her arms and said, 'Come and meet your new little sister.' I ran down the road full of excitement and saw the most beautiful little baby I had ever laid eyes on; she had tiny fingers and tiny toes and was already showing wispy blond curls. We all huddled round, me, my brothers, Auntie Frances and my granny, all cooing and fussing over the baby. It was a special day, a happy day for the whole family.

When Frances got a bit older my parents faced the slight problem of only having two bedrooms for a family with five children. But my father, always the optimist, quickly found a solution. He got together more friends from work and built a makeshift wall down the middle of the front bedroom. Frances and I shared one half and had a single bed each. The other half housed my parents' double bed, and a matching wardrobe and dresser, over which hung a beautiful mirror that we kids had to take turns dusting and cleaning. The wall itself was paper-thin but I didn't care. At that age I was thrilled to not have to share a bedroom with brothers, like so many other girls on my road had to do.

The three boys shared the other upstairs bedroom towards the back of the house. There were two fireplaces upstairs that my mother only lit on the coldest nights of winter or when one of us was sick.

The living room was on the first floor. I say living room because we did everything except sleep in that room. It was used as a kitchen, a dining room, and a general living area. My mother tried to separate the kitchen area by putting up a curtain, behind which was the big old Belfast sink and the cooker. We had a simple kitchen table and chairs, though my father had an old antique carver that he always sat in at the head of the table. Other than that, there was an armchair by the fire and Mammy's glass case. It was a wedding present that held all her prized possessions, like the cups she won for playing camogie, the medals we won for Irish dancing and her best china that was never used or taken out. It held everything that was important to her, like her wedding certificate and our birth certificates. It even had a lock on it.

We had a lot really, especially in comparison to other families around inner-city Dublin in the 1960s, and certainly in comparison to our own neighbours.

The house next door was chock-a-block with families in nearly every room. The Murphys, the Quinns, the O'Briens and the Gilmartins. I used to see Mrs O'Brien washing the sheets regularly outside at the tap. She had these huge muscles, gained it seemed from years of wringing out bedclothes. She was often joined by Mrs Murphy, who seemed always to be peeling potatoes. There was another family that lived in a little one-room extension at the back of that house. It was like a shed, really. I remember watching the children through the bars on their window. Their father never seemed to be around; he was either away in the army or at the pub. The mother was a very tall, good-looking girl who had six babies, one after the other, and she never seemed to be there either. The older children would often be left alone to take care of the younger ones. At that age they did the best they could but I would often see the babies walking around with no nappies on, naked from the waist down; they would drink from old Guinness bottles or jam jars with teats on them. As a child I thought our family was rich and they were poor. But as I got older I realized we were all poor on Charlemont Street, there were just different levels of poverty. There's one thing I will say: though many of us were poor, there was joy there, and a certain camaraderie between the neighbours who would always try to help each other out if they were stuck. No matter how bad things were for one person, we always knew there was somebody who was worse off.

In our house, Miss Brady lived in the downstairs room behind the shop, which she ran until she couldn't manage it any more. She was the oldest person I'd ever seen, a tiny little woman with grey hair tied back in a bun. She was a kind, gentle soul. My mother was fond of her, which made me like her too. She never married and at age ninety she had no family left of her own, so Mammy took it upon herself to take care of her. I remember as a child dreading being sent down to take something to Miss Brady because when you went into her room there was a strong smell of wee and 'old person'. For the last few years of her life the old woman was bedridden and my mother would take her dinner to her every evening. That was the sort of person my mother was. She looked after people, even people who weren't nice to her. She would say, 'Sure God help them, they've nobody.' When she was over eighty years old and living in Wolseley Street she would take care of her neighbour Mary. She would do day-to-day things for her, like getting her shopping and her newspaper, or she'd just sit with her to keep her company. She would tell me she would often call in and find Mary had fallen and she would pick her up off the floor without help from others. I used to give out to her when I heard this. 'Mammy, you're eighty-four! You're too old to be lifting people; you might hurt yourself! Call one of us and we'll come and help you.'

But Mammy couldn't bear to see someone in need and not help them. 'Ah, sure she was on the floor, God love her. I had to help her.' Mammy was always a giver.

This giving mentality and neighbourliness was prevalent among many of the women on Charlemont Street and in Dublin generally at that time. One particular instance of the kindness of those women stuck with me for life.

I was about six and it was Christmas morning. There was great excitement in our house because Santa Claus had come and I had got a scooter. I also got a new little doll, which I was given every year. I never understood why Santa Claus gave me a doll. I thought he should know that I didn't like playing with dolls; I was more of a tomboy. I found out later that it was because my mother loved dolls.

Later that morning, we all donned our new Christmas clothes and shoes and walked across to St Kevin's Church on Harrington Street for Christmas mass. The turkey was in the oven when we left and everything was prepared for the feast that we'd have later that day. As always it was a long mass with choirs and singing, and it felt all the longer to me and all the other children as our thoughts were back home with our toys from Santa. On the way home from mass we turned the corner on to Charlemont Street and saw two fire engines parked on the road and a group of people standing near our house.

Mammy looked really worried and whispered, 'Jesus, I hope that's not our house on fire.' As we got closer we realized that the firemen were running in and out of our front door, which had smoke billowing out of it. Our oven had caught fire. We all stood around outside watching helplessly. Mammy started crying and Daddy and the neighbours tried to console her.

'Wouldn't it have been worse if you and the children were in the house,' said Mrs Moore.

'It'll be all right, Patty,' said Mrs Lawlor.

'Sure, thank God nobody was hurt,' whispered Miss Sinnott.

When the fire engines left we followed Mammy through the front door, up the stairs and into the kitchen. The place was devastated. Everything had a film of black soot on it, including, to my horror, all my toys from Santa. The kitchen was the worst. It was covered in the yellowy white foam that was used to put the fire out. The Christmas dinner was ruined, of course, and there would be days of cleaning to be done. My mother stood there in silence staring at the room for quite a while.

Soon, though, the neighbours came around one by one. Some brought slices of turkey, some brought ham, others brought vegetables and potatoes; our neighbours wouldn't let us go without on Christmas Day. Miss Sinnott brought in half a Christmas pudding while Mrs Lawlor grabbed a clean cloth and washed down the table and some cutlery so we had somewhere to eat. Despite the horror of that morning, thanks to our neighbours, we still had a good Christmas and I'll never forget the generosity of those families. Although they had very little, they were still more than happy to share what they had with us.

2

'Songs of Pleasure and of Love'

MY MOTHER, JOSEPHINE Patricia Daly, was born in 1916 and reared on Eugene Street just off Cork Street in the Liberties in inner-city Dublin. She was the third of four children, two girls and two boys.

There weren't many pictures of my mother in her early life, but as a child I always thought she was beautiful; I loved her face. Looking at the pictures she did have, she was a very attractive woman when she was young. She never wore make-up except on the few occasions when she was going somewhere special, and then she'd put on a little Pond's dark red lipstick. On those occasions, I thought she was the height of glamour.

She had sandy brown shoulder-length hair with a soft wave in it that she usually wore clipped back at the sides. She wasn't what you'd call heavy, but she was a strong-looking woman, with big muscles from working hard. Mammy was like my granny in personality; she was a big softy. Her older sister, on the other hand, our auntie

Frances, was quite different. While we knew she had a soft centre, she had a crusty skin on the outside. She was six years older than Mammy and was never afraid to say a harsh word to someone. But she was very generous, kind and good. She really helped my mother during the tough times when she was trying to raise us. Auntie Frances's husband, a man called Lar Byrne, was from Bray in Co. Wicklow. He worked on the golf course out there, keeping the grounds. There was a very bad storm when he was on the grounds one night and a tree fell on him and broke his back. He was rushed to hospital and died a week later. Auntie Frances was absolutely heartbroken. They had only been married for three years. She moved back in with Granny and Mammy, who was still unmarried at the time.

Mammy and Frances shared a bed at Granny's house and Mammy often told the story of how, six months after Uncle Lar's death, Mammy woke up in the middle of the night and saw Lar standing over Frances, looking down at her. She always said she remembered it as clear as day and it was only in later years that she told Auntie Frances about it. When she did, Auntie Frances turned white.

Frances never remarried and in later years, when I asked her why, she told me, 'A widow never marries again.' It just wasn't done back then and to her it wouldn't have been the proper thing to do.

She worked all her life in Marlowe's Cleaners, and as

she had no family dependent on her, she gave whatever spare money she had to us to pay for our clothes, shoes and other necessities, or she would give Mammy a few extra bob if she was stuck. I often thought that maybe she lived with a broken heart for the rest of her life and that was why she had a hardened exterior.

Music was something Mammy loved all the way through her life. In her youth, all the neighbours would come together outside her house, where Granny would play the concertina, and there would be singing and dancing in the street during long summer evenings. She absolutely loved Irish dancing but her parents couldn't afford to send her to lessons as a child or pay for the dance costume that went with them. Instead she used to follow her friends to their dance lessons and watch through the keyhole, taking in all the steps and movements as they were taught. She learned all the dances that way. If, when the girls came out of the class, they had forgotten some of the steps, Mammy was able to demonstrate them again. She was a great dancer, very light on her feet and full of energy. After a while the dance teacher noticed her peeping through the keyhole and dancing with the girls after class and she invited her into the classroom to learn the dances for free. As she couldn't afford the costumes she was never allowed to take part with the other girls in competitions. But that didn't matter to Mammy, she was happy just to dance.

She left school at fourteen and got her first job delivering milk to the wealthier houses on South Circular Road. Back then they delivered milk churns not bottles, so every morning from five o'clock she would carry four milk churns, deliver them, then go back to the dairy house and get four more. Backbreaking work, but she managed it somehow, even at that young age. She later got a job in the Rowntree's chocolate factory. It was a big employer in the area at the time and many of her neighbours worked alongside her.

The work itself was easier than delivering milk but it had its downside; Mammy gained three stone in six months. She couldn't resist eating the chocolate! Her job was to put the cream into the walnut whips.

The foremen at the factory all loved to have Mammy on their shift because she would start up a song, all the women would join in, and somehow their work would become much more productive. Mammy sang everywhere she went. It was part and parcel of who she was. She'd burst into song and then all the other girls would join in and the work would just flow. They were content in their singing, forgetting all about the work itself, and they would slot into a rhythm with one another through the rhythm of the song. The work was always done far better when Mammy was there leading the singing.

Before she left work every evening she'd quietly splash as much chocolate as she could on her apron, which she'd have to bring home to clean. When she arrived home there'd be a horde of children from the street gathered around her door, all-bustling to get their piece of chocolate, which she'd scrape off her apron into a bag and share out among them.

My mother's love of dance remained with her as she grew up; she loved going to dances and used to sing at the interval. It was an informal thing; people would get up and sing at the break, but they soon got to know Mammy. She had a good voice and would be invited up to sing at every dance. She did it purely for pleasure, of course, there was no payment involved. That was the closest she got to singing to an audience, and I know she would have loved to do more of that.

My mother enjoyed her youth as much as any working-class woman back then and didn't meet my father until she was thirty. Being thirty and single wasn't a big deal then, not to my mother anyway. In later years when I asked her if she was ever worried that she'd be left on the shelf she said, 'Not at all, sure I was having a great time!' She'd had serious relationships with two men before my father; sadly, one of them died, and the other broke her heart.

The first guy was a friend of Auntie Frances's husband, Lar. Mammy and her cousin Sheila would often go out to visit Frances in Bray and during one trip there she was introduced to her first boyfriend. He was a lovely young lad and Mammy fell fast and she would often spend her Saturdays visiting him out in Bray. However, one week she got a letter from him to say that he was sick and asked her not to come and visit him that weekend. He had tonsillitis. The following week she got another letter to say that she must come out immediately as he was seriously ill and he wanted to see her. When she saw him his tongue had swollen to the point that it was protruding out of his mouth and he was gasping for air; he was actually choking on his tonsils. He could hardly speak to her when he arrived but he knew he was very ill and just wanted to see her before he died. He died two days later. Mammy was in bits afterwards, heartbroken really.

A few years after this, when she was still only in her early twenties, she met a fella called Davey Bolger from Wexford.

He was working in Dublin when he met Mammy, and she fell for him straight away because he was a great dancer. Things were going well between them for about a year or so, until his father died and his mother ordered him to come home to take care of the family farm. So he went back to Wexford. He said he'd write to her and keep in touch, which he did for a little while until she got the letter that said he had met someone else from the area. It absolutely broke her heart. She said she cried for a year after it, and didn't dance or sing once in that time.

After that she nearly gave up on men in a way, until she met my dad.

One night her best friend Ettie was going to a dinner dance on a blind date with a man a mutual friend had set her up with. At the last minute Ettie got sick and asked Mammy to go in her place. Mammy wasn't keen but when Ettie offered to lend her the lovely dress, bag and shoes she had bought specially for the occasion, Mammy changed her mind. She was thrilled at the thought of dressing up in all those new clothes for the night!

The man she met that night was my father, Kevin Black from Rathlin Island, Co. Antrim. He was a plasterer and was much sought after around Dublin as he was left-handed, which meant he could easily restore areas that right-handed plasterers found difficult. He was particularly talented at restoring old cornice plasterwork.

However, his real passion was music. He played the fiddle, banjo and mandolin, none of them brilliantly, but he had a wealth of tunes and songs that he shared with customers around the pubs of Dublin in the evenings.

When Daddy first arrived in Dublin city he hopped on a number 20 bus and asked the bus conductor where he could get digs. The conductor pointed him in the direction of Charlemont Street, where he stayed for over forty years. He spent ten years enjoying the single life in Dublin before he met my mother.

The night they met they hit it off straight away and

started seeing each other often. I think it was their mutual love of music that really drew them towards each other. Daddy loved her outgoing personality and the fact that she would sing at the drop of a hat. And Mammy always said she couldn't resist his Northern accent.

Daddy was thirty-nine when he met my mother, but even at this mature age it didn't mean he had the right to marry her without his parents' blessing. Before he could pop the question she had to be brought up to Rathlin to be checked over for approval. Of course, Mammy charmed them with her singing and dancing and her good sense of humour, and she was a good-looking woman into the bargain. Mammy's parents approved of Dad too. Her father worked on the building sites and was able to do a check on him through other workers. He soon found out that he was a good worker and a popular man among the men he worked with.

Mammy always told me my father never actually asked her to marry him. One day he just said to her, in his thick Antrim accent: 'There comes a time in every man's life when he has to build his nest . . .' and the next thing she knew she found herself in a jewellery shop picking out a ring with her new fiancé. She never said yes, and she never said no, she just went along with it.

They were married on the third of August 1949. Shay came along in September 1950, so they didn't hang about in the building-a-family department. Things were tight enough in the beginning but they were able to manage and soon made a home for themselves in one room of number 69 Charlemont Street.

3

'God Bless the Child'

I WAS LUCKY as a child; my parents, especially Mammy, knew the value of a decent education and wanted me to go to a good school. They knew that St Louis Primary in Rathmines had a good reputation and felt it would be better for me to go there than the local schools, like Grantham Street Primary or Warren Mount, where all the other girls on our street went. As I've already said, money was tight, but my parents managed to scrape up enough money to pay for my uniform, the shoes and all the other bits and pieces you needed to have to go to St Louis. I remember feeling very proud knowing that I was the only girl on my street who was going to St Louis, and it wasn't until later that I realized that where I came from would be something some of my classmates and teachers would hold against me in school.

That first morning, after putting on my uniform as carefully as I could, I walked hand in hand with my mother out the door of our house in Charlemont Street and made the short journey over the canal and through Rathmines village to my new school. I was nervous as I walked up the stone steps of St Louis Primary, tightly clutching my mother's hand. I remember vividly the hustle and bustle of all the mothers and children around us. Some girls were crying, some were running around the hallways, but most, like me, were quietly holding on to their mother's hand for dear life.

I had with me, like all the other children, my cloth bag in which we were told to have a little towel, a bar of soap and two dusters. I loved that little bar of soap. At home we only had a huge bar of Lifebuoy soap which was used to wash everything – including the dishes, the floors and us! I soon discovered that the towel and soap were to clean our hands and face when we were in school because, of course, the school didn't have the funds to provide them. Every other day the dusters were strapped to our stockinged feet and, in a line across the corridors, we would clean the floors of the school by 'skating' along the halls.

We were eventually directed down the long corridor to room 4 – my new classroom. The mixture of nerves and excitement was rising in my chest; soon I would be with my new classmates and my new teacher, something I had been looking forward to all summer. Soon, too, I knew I would have to say goodbye to the comforting presence that was my mammy. I would have to try not to cry when she left because we didn't do that in our family. We weren't really huggers, or kissers; back then we didn't tell each other we loved one another. This day was no exception. As we walked towards the classroom door I looked up at my mother's face; she had clipped back her sandy brown shoulder-length hair, and wore her usual overcoat over a simple dress. Her expression was calm. As children we weren't really coddled or praised but I really felt my mother was proud of me that day, even though she never said it; I had been accepted into a good school and, so far, I'd held up well and not broken down in tears.

When Mammy and me entered the classroom we joined the line of mothers and children waiting to meet the nun who would be my teacher for the next three years.

When we reached the top of the queue there stood the looming figure of Sister Norbert. She had a huge smile on her face, framed squarely by her white head-dress and covered again by a tall black veil. The only skin visible was that small square face and her tiny hands; the rest of her was draped in black. She came towards me like a huge black angel, stretching her arms out to give me a big hug. All I could see were these black wings enveloping me; rosary beads swinging menacingly towards me like a metal chain. That's when the tears came, silently.

I was later to realize that that smile of hers left her

face the second the parents left the room. She had a wicked temper.

From the time I was a baby I had recurring ear infections which affected my hearing. As a result of these infections I missed a lot of school those first two years. I remember how extremely painful it was and when it got really bad I would have yellow gunge seeping from my ear. My mother was constantly going to the doctor to get me antibiotics for this problem.

They eventually discovered that the reason for all the infections was my tonsils. When I was in senior infants, I was finally taken to hospital to sort it out. I clearly remember my mammy taking me to the hospital and clinging to her skirt when I realized she was going to leave me there. She told me that I was to be a big girl and not to cry. To make me feel better she bought me a little bar of Cadbury's chocolate. I couldn't believe I was getting this chocolate all to myself so I tried really, really hard not to cry. But as she walked out, waved to me and smiled, I looked down and noticed the bar of chocolate was melting in my hand. The tears started then.

I was only in hospital for a couple of days getting my tonsils out but I was very sick after it. Back in those days there was no staying in hospital all day with your sick child. Parents came in to see you during visiting hours and that was it. Before long, though, I was back on my feet and home, and the ear infections cleared up.

In school, before the tonsils operation, I would often get into trouble with Sister Norbert for 'not listening' in class. The truth was I just couldn't hear properly. One day she asked me a question, but I didn't hear her. I remember looking down at the book we were reading and I didn't see or hear her creeping down the aisle of desks towards me until she brought the bata down on my hands with all her strength. The bata was the round wooden stick she used for pointing to the blackboard; more often than not this doubled up as a disciplinary tool. The pain was vicious. But I sucked it up, as we all did in those days.

I don't know why but I didn't tell Mammy when I got home. At that point I thought this was the norm in school and had begun to believe that I was in the wrong and deserved to be hit. Usually though, Sister Norbert would hit us with the ruler across the head or back, which didn't leave a mark like the bata did. A few days after the bata incident I was sitting having tea with my brothers and my mother asked me, 'What's all that dirt on your hands, Mary?' I still have the image of looking down at the back of my little baby hands and seeing two strips of black bruises across each one. My mother walked to the sink to get a damp cloth and kneeled down to clean the 'dirt' off.

'Mother of God, they're bruises! What happened to

ye?' When I told her Sister Norbert hit me with the bata because I didn't hear her question she started to pace up and down the kitchen. She was absolutely fuming. 'Hitting a small child!', 'A grown woman!', 'Who does she think . . . !' and 'With a bata!' were a few phrases she came out with while we had our tea.

When Daddy came home from work she burst into the story. 'Kevin! You won't believe what that nun has done to our Mary!' My father, ever the peacekeeper, hated any kind of fighting or confrontation and tried to calm my mother down. But Mammy had a temper too and wouldn't let it rest. 'How dare she? I'm going up to that school tomorrow and I'm going to tear the veil off that nun!'

But Daddy persisted. 'Ah, Patsy, Patsy! Don't go up there, you'll only make it worse for the child!' Mammy eventually calmed down and agreed that she wouldn't make a scene, but she went up to the school the next day and politely told Sister Norbert that I had a hearing problem, which was why I wasn't responding to her in class. As for Sister Norbert, she made sure she didn't leave a mark on me again. She only used the ruler after that episode.

4

'Schooldays Over'

LIFE IN IRELAND in the 1960s was difficult for many. There was little work to be had, people didn't have money to splash around and emigration was at a high. Luckily for us Daddy was rarely out of work. He was good at his job, worked hard and was popular with his bosses. Sometimes, when work was scarce, he would have to travel to find jobs around the country, and he'd have to pay for digs, which meant less money coming into the house. With a family of five kids, Mammy found it hard to make ends meet back at home and in order to put food on the table she got a job cleaning offices, from 5.30 to 9.30 every evening.

At the age of eight, as the eldest girl in the family, it fell to me to mind the house and make sure everybody got their tea on time. When Daddy came home from work it was my job to give him his dinner. Even though there were times when I wanted to be playing out on the street with my friends, I kind of enjoyed the role of housekeeper and all the duties and responsibilities I'd been given.

It was strange not having Mammy around the house at first. She had always been there when we were home and in the beginning the prospect of taking on her mantle, if only for a few hours a day, was quite daunting. I have to say, however, that being in charge at that young age also instilled in me a sense of responsibility. My family was relying on me and I realized that I could take on some of my mother's duties. It gave me a quiet confidence and I think it was about then that I began to feel that I could do anything if I put my mind to it, something which stood me in good stead when I was older.

I particularly loved it when Daddy came home and I'd hand him his dinner. He'd say, 'Ach, aren't you the great girl, able to do that at your age.'

It was a great feeling getting praise from my father. He'd always give praise when it was due. He had a very gentle way about him and hated violence of any sort. So much so, when my brothers wanted to play cowboys and Indians they weren't allowed to have toy guns.

If they ever made toy swords from sticks they would be swiftly broken over my father's knee, thrown in the fire and with a final word he'd say, 'There'll be no knives in this house.' He never raised a hand to us, which was rare for parents back then, and he never even raised his voice. The most he would ever say if he wanted a bit of peace and quiet so that he could listen to the news was, 'Whisht!' and maybe bang the newspaper on the table.

My brother Michael had the same gentle nature as Dad. He was two and a half years older than me and we always got along well. I had an extra soft spot for him because he had red hair and freckles – not always a popular combination then or now – and he had to endure a lot of mickey-taking and name-calling, such as 'Carrot Top', 'Ginger' or 'Redser'. Michael was also sensitive to the hardships my parents went through. While we all did the jobs we were asked to do around the house, Michael would offer to help even after his chores were done.

He was bright in school too, and loved sports. Back then Synge Street was a fee-paying school but Michael sat a Dublin Corporation exam and won a scholarship. This meant the fees were waived and the books were provided for. That scholarship amounted to £40 per year, which was paid in two instalments. It was meant to buy his uniform and some more books, but sometimes there would be some money left over to buy basic necessities for the home. I don't know how Mammy managed to stretch that money, but somehow she did.

At that time my dad would often slip out to meet some of the local men in the pub when he finished work. One evening he got talking to Ronnie Elliott, who was employed by Guinness's and lived in the Ffrench Mullen Flats across the street from us. Ronnie convinced my father that getting a job in the Guinness brewery was a great opportunity for anyone looking. So, after just two years in Synge Street Secondary School, and not long after Michael's thirteenth birthday, when an opportunity arose to take an examination to gain entry into Guinness's my parents had Michael take the test.

At that time the Guinness brewery was a thriving commercial success in Dublin, employing over three thousand people. It was widely known that if you got a job there you were paid well, got free medical insurance, had the opportunity to rise through the ranks of the company and they would also provide you with a pension at the end of it all. It was a coveted job among the working class because the company offered job security. Anyone who landed a job at Guinness's was considered to be set for life.

Michael passed the exam with flying colours but now faced the decision of whether to stay at school or leave and start work at the age of just fourteen. This was difficult for Michael; he was doing well in school and wasn't sure if leaving was the right choice for him. However, everyone urged him to go for the job. Our parents told him that it was his decision to make, but he knew they thought it was an opportunity he shouldn't pass up. As I said, times were fairly tough back then and a secure job with prospects was not something to be dismissed without serious consideration. Any adult he asked for advice about it would say, 'You'd be mad not to go to Guinness's.' Though it was never spoken of, I think Michael knew that getting this job would bring more money into the house and it would make things easier on the family. So, although it was his decision, he felt the pressure from all sides and eventually decided to leave school.

Michael started work as a messenger boy at Guinness's and seemed happy enough at the beginning. He made friends quickly and was always coming home with funny stories about what his co-workers had said or done.

During this time he was learning how to play the guitar and the banjo and found others at work who shared an interest in music. He honed his skills as a player in sessions after work with friends like Jerry Lawes and Pat Good. He also developed a beautiful tenor voice that could instantly quieten a crowd when he started to sing.

After a few years in the job, Michael began to feel that maybe his decision to leave school had been the wrong one. I think he grew bored with the job, and when he saw the men who worked around him, some of whom had been working at Guinness's for fifty years, he realized that it wasn't the life he wanted for himself.

He began to study at night to take his Leaving Cert. exams. Unfortunately, he was also competing against full-time secondary school students and did not get the grades he so desperately needed to be accepted at Thomond College of Education, where he wanted to study Physical Education. He spent seven years trying to leave Guinness's so that he could begin a new career, and eventually when he was twenty-four he applied to some colleges in England.

He was accepted at St Mary's College of Education in Strawberry Hill, Twickenham, under a mature student programme. It was only the confirmation letter he received from the Registrar which ruined the moment and demonstrated a lack of confidence in Michael's ability to cope with the course given his nationality and working-class background. Michael still has the letter, which he has framed, which states:

I feel I must add that the department of Movement Studies is very hesitant about your ability to gain the Certificate of Education . . . and with your background it is very difficult to envisage your achieving this standard in three years.

This was like a red rag to a bull for Michael and made him even more determined. He accepted the offer and after three years he received his Certificate of Education.

He then went on to receive an Honours Degree from Thomond College of Education (now University of Limerick). Following this he taught in Balally Community School, Dublin for a year before applying for a Master's Degree programme at both the University of Southern California, Los Angeles, and the University of California, Berkeley. He was accepted at both but decided on Berkeley as he liked the feel of the San Francisco Bay area.

Michael arrived in San Francisco with a haversack on his shoulder and a banjo and guitar in hand, knowing nobody and with very little money. He eventually found the Plough and Stars Irish Pub on Geary Boulevard and asked the boss if he could audition to get a spot singing and playing tunes. The boss, Sean Heaney, was impressed and offered him as many gigs as he wanted. Those gigs opened numerous doors for him and he became heavily involved in the Irish music scene in San Francisco. If it hadn't been for this work, he would not have survived financially while studying at Berkeley.

Michael received his Master's Degree in Physical Education after three years and completed a Ph.D. in Human Biodynamics in 1996. It became quite an adventure for him and he told me many times that he had a tough time keeping up with his studies, playing gigs and generally trying to earn enough to pay for his school fees, food and rent.

Whenever I visited Michael, that initial letter of acceptance was prominently displayed in whatever flat he happened to be living in. It became the sole motivation for proving to himself that, despite his working-class Dublin background, and having left school at fourteen, he could achieve academic success. In fact, upon receiving his doctorate degree he composed a short note which he sent to the Registrar's office back in St Mary's College. He felt he needed to do it as a way of coming full circle. The letter read:

Dear Registrar,

Please find enclosed the acceptance letter you wrote to me in July 1977. I would ask you to note the highlighted sections regarding my supposed inability to achieve Certificate status in Education. I am happy to report to you that I proved you wrong and that inadvertently, you provided me with the drive to achieve my life-long goals. Perhaps this note serves as a reminder that there are times in one's life where we should look beyond the prejudice of class and race and instead focus on will, desire and perseverance.

Yours sincerely,

Dr. Michael Black, Cert. Ed. (Hons.), B. Ed. (Hons.), M.A., Ph.D.

When Michael received his degree from Limerick at the age of thirty we couldn't have been more proud of him. He was the first person in our family to complete third-level education and for someone who'd left school at fourteen this was a huge achievement. I looked up to him so much. He'd followed his dream and never gave up, no matter how tough things were for him. I was about twenty when he went to England to get his degree. At that time I had just completed a secretarial course and was working in a wool shop in Molesworth Street. I hated the secretarial course and didn't particularly like the wool shop either. Seeing Michael fulfil his goals inspired me to take control of my own life and what I wanted from it. If he could break away from the confines of the limited expectations placed on him, why couldn't I? It was then that I began to look at the one thing that I loved and which I knew I could do well, and that was singing; I seriously considered making a career out of it, and although there were no guarantees that I would succeed, I knew that, just like Michael, I would have to try.

If Michael was a bit of a hero to me when I was young, Shay was the one we all looked up to as kids. He was the eldest child in the family and paved the way with his love of music. He was also the first one of us to pick up an instrument and play a song.

Shay had a great passion for music and started to collect songs from an early age. When we were growing up in the 1960s, bands like The Clancy Brothers and The Dubliners made folk ballads popular. But Shay, while he liked these bands, endeavoured to find more obscure traditional folk songs. He, too, got a scholarship to Synge Street, where he got his Leaving Cert., and went on to study Maritime Radio Technology at Kevin Street Technical College. When he was about twenty-one he decided to emigrate to England to get work.

After spending time in Canterbury, Kent, and Hampstead and Camberwell in London, Shay settled in Liverpool. I think he missed Ireland and thought that the Irish scene in Liverpool would be more welcoming to him. It was also just a hop, skip and a jump from Ireland and he hoped to be able to get back to Dublin more frequently.

It was quite a wrench when he left because he was the first of the family to leave home. Back then England seemed very far away and we knew we might not see him again for a long time. With no telephone in the house we could only get in touch through letters and the local phone box. For years after he left, he would sometimes call that public telephone box on Charlemont Street, and some passerby would run into the house to get Mammy to tell her Shay was on the phone. The day he left we all got the train with him to Dun Laoghaire. Standing on the pier waving goodbye as his ferry pulled away seemed very final at the time.

When we were young our personalities clashed and Shay and I fought a lot. For all the boys on the street, there was an expectation that they would tease their little sisters, and he would know exactly how to bait me until I was in a rage. He found it highly amusing to wind me up and thought it was very funny when I got angry with him. This in turn would make me even madder and I would try to punch him to stop him laughing. However, as he was always five years older than me and usually a foot taller, he would simply hold my head in one hand at arm's length while I swung madly at his torso. I rarely landed a blow, but I gave it a good try!

One day when Mammy was out, Shay and me were in the kitchen and he was pushing my buttons more than usual. I was about eight and he was thirteen, and he had an arsenal of taunts he'd picked up from joking with his teenage friends all day. After one comment I couldn't take it any more. My eyes shot to the knife on the kitchen table and without a second thought I flung it across the room at him. It struck him above his right eye and he immediately put his hand to where he was hit. He took his hand away and there was blood everywhere. He looked at me in utter shock and before he could bring himself to speak Mammy walked in.

'What's going on here?' She looked at me and then at Shay, blood running down his face.

I ran. My survival instinct kicked in and I sprinted past her up the stairs to the only room in the house with a lock. The toilet.

I could hear Shay downstairs telling on me in a teary voice. 'She's after throwing a knife at me!'

Then came the heavy footsteps on the stairs and the stern voice, 'Come down here now.' I didn't respond and curled myself into a ball in the corner of the toilet. When she realized I had locked myself in she came all the way up the stairs and stood outside the door.

In a slow, calm, low voice she commanded, 'Open. This. Door.' I could hear the restraint in her voice when she spoke and I knew she was holding back the anger.

'No, you'll hit me!' I screamed.

'Open. This. Door,' was the only reply.

'No!'

'Mary Black, open this door now!' A little faster now.

My mind raced. I knew I would have to face her sooner or later and there was no prospect of an immediate escape because the window was too small for me to squeeze out. Slowly I got up off the floor, slid the lock open and pushed myself to the far corner of the toilet. She was standing sideways to the left of the door, leaving a pathway open for me to get by with her hand pointing down the hall.

'Get down them stairs,' she snapped in the same restrained voice.

I knew I was in serious trouble and tried to make a run for it. But she was too quick for me. She caught me with a clatter on the back of the head as I ran past her.

She ran down the stairs after me, landing a few more wallops to the back of my legs and shouting, 'Don't you ever throw anything like that again.'

I never did. It took me a while to forgive Shay, though; I didn't talk to him for about two weeks, which was donkey's years at that age. I think he realized how much his teasing really upset me as it became less incessant after the knife incident, or maybe he was just worried I'd throw something else at him.

As I've said, though we had our disagreements as kids, music was the one thing that brought us together. Shay recognized my talent as a singer at a young age, long before I did, and he nurtured it as we grew up. He always encouraged me to learn new songs, to project my voice confidently and sing with feeling. He found songs that he thought I would be well able for and that suited my voice. He'd then hand me the lyrics and teach me how to sing them while he backed me on guitar. This proved to be invaluable to me as a performer when I got older. Without even knowing it, I had developed my own style from an early stage and had a repertoire of songs that were not the popular ballads that everyone knew.

Shay is still as passionate now about music as he ever was. He's been living in Berkeley, California for the last twenty years and has immersed himself in the music scene of the Bay area. He performs and teaches singing in folk repertoire classes, and with Michael also living in the area the two of them get together and perform as The Black Brothers. He has two beautiful daughters, Anna and Shosí.

5

Hey little brother . . .

MY BROTHER MARTIN came along when I was about two and a half years old. Of all my siblings he was the one who looked most like me with black curly hair, sallow skin and eyelashes like spider legs. Though his eyes were blue and mine green, we were the two kids that had the look of my father.

Martin was a healthy baby when he was born, ten fingers and ten toes just like everyone else. But when he was about a year and a half he had a fit, a sort of convulsion. I remember Mammy running up Charlemont Street to St Ultan's Hospital with him in her arms.

Initially they thought he just had a high temperature, which they told my mother often happens with young kids, and that this is what had caused the fit. However, it began to happen a bit more regularly as he got older. When he was about six she took him down to the hospital in Harcourt Street to get him checked out.

After various tests the doctors told my mother that Martin had a weak heart and that he was 'delicate'. They said he would have to go to a convalescent hospital in Co. Dublin. It was a hospital for sick children and Mammy was told he would have to stay there for a long time.

It was heartbreaking for my mother. She, of course, went along with whatever these well-educated doctors and nurses had to tell her about her son, and didn't hesitate to follow their recommendations, even if it meant she could only visit Martin twice a week, on Wednesdays and Sundays, for an indefinite period of time.

On Sundays, the whole family would go out to visit him. It was really hard for poor Martin too; he was desperately lonely. It was like being in a boarding school, but he was never taught anything and wasn't allowed to leave his bed. He used to tell Mammy that the nurses would frighten him and the other children with stories of ghosts roaming around in the wards, to make them hide under the covers and go to sleep. If they didn't, they were told the monsters would get them. Martin even made his first Holy Communion out there.

Martin stayed for two years in that hospital, but seemed to receive no special treatment; he was just constantly 'monitored' as they called it. It turned out that the hospital received money from the government for every child that was in its care. Many believed that the hospitals purposely kept children in for as long as they could in order to receive the maximum funding, but at the time this was something my mother would never have suspected.

Eventually, after two years of Martin being bed-ridden, Mammy began to look for answers from the doctors. This might seem like it took a long time for a mother to act but you have to remember the times we were in. It was the early 1960s and we were a working-class family from the city; my mother, like so many others at the time, put her trust in the authorities and other professionals, such as doctors, for fear that her son might die. Back then child mortality was still a reality facing many parents every day.

But seeing her son living that way for so long Mammy finally plucked up the courage to challenge the hospital and asked the questions that many other mothers never did. What exactly was wrong with him? What treatment was he getting? Why was he in there?

She got no straight answers from anyone for weeks so she marched in one day and told them, 'I'm taking him home.'

Their response was along the lines of, 'Well, it'll be on your own head. If anything happens to him it won't be our responsibility.' This made her feel even more worried, of course, but she'd had enough. She stood her ground and took him home. It was the best thing she ever did for him because, as we later discovered, some children were kept in that place for years and years; they got no benefit whatsoever from being in there, and some had nothing wrong with them at all.

We never really got to the bottom of it but I read an article about it years later which told the stories of other children who'd had the same experience as Martin. They had been in that same hospital for most of their childhood but they turned out to have been perfectly healthy all along; they were just the victims of some financial scam.

When little Martin got out he was so overexcited to be home that he ran and ran all day long with the kids from the street. In fact, when the street heard the news that Martin Black was home from hospital they gave him a great welcome.

Unfortunately, Martin's running around proved too much for him and when he woke up the next morning he couldn't move his legs. Being bedridden for two years meant that his muscles couldn't handle all the exercise and he struggled to walk for two weeks after that.

I always got along well enough with Martin. I suppose we fought as much as any siblings would, especially when we hit our teens, but he was always a good honest kid and about a year or two after he got home from hospital he showed a degree of sibling loyalty and kindness I had never experienced before. It was something I will never forget.

I had been learning gymnastics at school and one day I invited young Martin into my room to teach him how to do a crab. For those of you who don't know, a crab is when you do a handstand and then fall backwards and land on your feet, chest facing the ceiling with your back arched and with your hands still touching the floor. Usually, well in my PE class anyway, someone would get down on their hands and knees and you'd do the crab over them. So I thought it was a great idea to try this with Martin. I told him to get down on his hands and knees and I'd show him how impressively I could do a crab over him. Like the good brother he was he complied without question. I then executed a perfect handstand only to fall straight down full force on top of Martin and in the process I broke his arm. I'll never forget the image of him lying in a heap on the floor with his arm bent back at an awkward and unnatural angle. He had a look of terrible pain on his face.

I shot up. 'Oh my God! I'll get Mammy.'

But he stopped me before I could reach the door.

'No, no! Come back, come back.'

I looked at him in disbelief. 'Why? What?'

He looked back with real concern. 'Don't tell her you were doing a handstand over me or she'll kill you!' He looked around the room quickly; during my performance a glass of water had been knocked off my bedside table. 'Tell her I slipped on the water and it was only an accident.' He was eight or nine at the time and I couldn't believe how brave and thoughtful he was being during this moment of agonizing pain.

Mammy believed our story and he was kept in hospital overnight. I cried all that night. The guilt I felt was unbelievable. I never told Mammy, even when I got older. I knew she'd still kill me no matter what age I was.

When we were teenagers Martin and I fought a lot. I suppose it was a mix of being close in age and hormones running high. He drove me mad and he thought I was a crazy person. When Joe proposed to me and we were planning for the wedding, Martin took him aside one day and asked him seriously, 'Are you sure you know what you're getting yourself into? Do you really know what she's like?' He was honestly concerned for Joe's well-being and thought he'd be miserable for the rest of his life if he married me!

On the day of Martin's eighteenth birthday he had a party to celebrate with his pals in the house and they all slept over. They were sleeping in the living room on the couches, or wherever they could find a comfortable spot. The next morning someone rang the doorbell and Martin jumped off the couch and came bounding down the stairs, two at a time, to answer it. When he got to the bottom of the stairs he went into a fit. We got him to hospital as fast as we could and it was then that they finally diagnosed him with epilepsy. That was the first of his adult epileptic fits and it is something he has lived with since.

Martin has a great attitude and he has never let his illness affect the way he lives his life. He has pursued his love of music, and recorded his own solo album after recording and touring with The Black Family and The Black Brothers. He has four beautiful children, Sara, Emily, Kevin and Michael. He now works in Dublin City Libraries, although music is still an important part of his life. I don't believe we have ever discovered whether his epilepsy had a connection with his childhood convulsions or not; we just can't be sure, although most likely it was the case and it just didn't show up on any of his tests.

Through it all, and despite this health problem, he's always had a very positive and optimistic attitude towards life. I greatly admire the way Martin has coped with the difficult cards he's been dealt.

Her simple smile is Heaven's gate . . .
I am crouching near the door in the kitchen of my home in Charlemont Street. Mammy stands at the other end of the room, in her slippers and her well-worn apron,

holding out her index fingers in front of her. Clasping on to both fingers are the hands of my little sister. It is the summer time and she is wearing a pair of cotton pantaloons and a lemon blouse over her freckled tanned skin.

I crouch down further on to my honkers, grinning, and stretch out my arms towards her, 'Come on, Frances, come on, you can do it!'

She looks up at me with her startling blue eyes, her blond curls bouncing, and smiles at the sight of me. She is the opposite of me in so many ways with my black hair, green eyes and sallow skin, but when we smile you can see we share our mother's high cheekbones. She takes an uneasy step forward but keeps her gaze on me. With her second step she lets go of one of my mother's fingers, holding her hand in the air for balance. With her third step she is standing on her own and doesn't realize it. Mammy and I hold our breath in silent anticipation. She takes another step and another until she is almost running the length between us, picking up momentum as she goes, and it looks like she is about to fall. I catch her in my open arms just before she does. Mammy and I cheer for her enthusiastically.

'Hooray! Hooray! You're such a big girl!' I shout as I jostle her in my arms.

I am six years old and I love my little sister.

* * *

61

Being the youngest, Frances was much loved in our house as a baby. We didn't play together the same way I played with my brothers when we were kids because of the five-year age gap. It was only when she reached her teens that Frances became a bit wild and started hanging out with a gang from school. And when she got to the age where she started going out on her own with her friends that's when the trouble really started between us. She would take my clothes from my wardrobe and wear them without asking; she'd also sneak out with my shoes even though she was a half size bigger than me and would stretch them until they were ruined. This used to drive me crazy and there would be murder in the house when I found one of my new tops or some other item of clothing in a heap at the bottom of her bed after she'd worn it on a night out. This happened time and time again but she didn't seem to care.

It got to the point where I put a lock on my wardrobe, although it took her less than a week to break into it and run off with my best outfit. When I discovered the broken lock and missing clothes we had the mother of all rows and Mammy had to hold me back from her. It was just the usual teenage differences, though, and despite these skirmishes I still tried to look out for her and watch who she was hanging out with and where she was going. Mammy was naïve and unaware of Frances's antics so I made sure I was on top of things.

One night when I was about twenty I came home and walked into the kitchen to find her and Mammy sitting by the fire. Frances had a bandage around her hand.

'What happened?' I asked, looking at the bandage.

'She took a weakness and fell into the fire,' Mammy said innocently.

I took one look at Frances and knew that she was drunk. It would never even have dawned on Mammy that her darling little fifteen-year-old was drinking. I said nothing to Mammy, but brought Frances up to our bedroom and told her she hadn't fooled me. I gave her a good talking to that night. I always tried to be vigilant where Frances was concerned, although at times I'm sure it became irritating to have me nagging on about who she was with and what she was doing. But, like me, she was strong-willed and had a mind of her own; she'd often tell me, 'You're not my mother.'

We fought like sisters usually do growing up, but, of course, we did love each other. But I don't think it was until we were both a little older and I was moving out of home that Frances and I became really good friends.

I asked her to be my bridesmaid at my wedding. She was nineteen when I got married. Even on my wedding day we rowed about some piece of underwear of mine that she had taken! Unusually, though, she started crying after I yelled at her. I thought it was a bit strange; she wasn't usually that dramatic and didn't normally dissolve into tears when we argued. It wasn't until a little while later that we discovered why she was feeling more sensitive than usual.

Frances had been with her boyfriend Richard for a few years and shortly after my wedding she found out she was pregnant.

When she told my parents they were very upset, especially my dad. He grew up in a different era and to him it was the height of shame to be told your unmarried daughter was pregnant. Even though Mammy was upset, she made it clear from the outset that she would support Frances through it.

It was March 1980 and my parents had been running the shop on Charlemont Street for about seven years. When our neighbour Miss Brady got too old, the shop at the front of our house was left idle for many years. When Daddy retired the two of them decided to reopen it as Black's General Grocers. Around this time Frances's bump started to show and Daddy, embarrassed and ashamed, told her to come in and out of the back door of the house instead of through the shop where the neighbours would see her. I can only imagine how this made Frances feel. I thought it was a ridiculous request, and although Mammy was more compassionate about Frances's situation, she stood by Daddy in his decision. I think the fact that Mammy didn't stick up for Frances about this upset her the most.

One day soon after, there was another upsetting incident. Frances came home from the crèche where she worked to find Daddy waiting for her in the back yard. He said that Uncle John, his brother, had arrived unexpectedly and that she couldn't come into the house. He said they'd give her a bag of her things and she'd have to stay somewhere else until Uncle John left.

Frances moved in with Richard's mother, who was a lovely woman, until Uncle John left a few days later. My father left Dublin soon after that to attend his sister Maggie's funeral in Co. Down and he didn't come back until after the baby was born – about three months later. I don't think my father could handle the 'shame'. That upset my mother a lot. Although she too felt shame I think she thought he should face up to the problem rather than run away from it or pretend it wasn't happening. It was the only time I was ever disappointed in my father and more than a little angry with him, although I also understood that he was raised in a culture and at a time that was dominated by the Catholic Church and by what I considered were hypocritical and old-fashioned attitudes. Everything was based on shame, guilt and sin – not to mention the hellfire and damnation that followed if you strayed from the path of righteousness!

Frances was young and had fallen into a difficult situation, and she needed to know that she was loved and that her baby would be welcome in our family. And that's exactly what we did. Beautiful little Eoghan was born in November 1980 and we all fell instantly in love with him. Frances and Eoghan moved in with me and Joe in our house off South Circular Road for a while after Eoghan was born.

When Daddy came home he was distant with Eoghan at first and my parents put Frances and Richard under a lot of pressure to get married after Eoghan's birth. In their eyes it was the right thing to do. Daddy told Frances that he could never accept Eoghan as his grandson unless she got married to Richard. They were married the following May. I was her bridesmaid and pregnant with Conor at the time.

Frances was pregnant again when she was twenty-one, and his time, when little Aoife was born, there were complications after the birth. Frances had internal bleeding and the doctors couldn't find where it was coming from. At one stage her heartbeat slowed to the minimum and she was losing blood by the pint.

Frances told me later of a vision she'd had that day. A man appeared to her, a man who she felt oddly drawn to; he was coming to take her away. He showed her the faces of her loved ones so she could say goodbye as they travelled towards a bright light. Mammy and I flashed in front of her before finally Eoghan and Aoife's little faces appeared. At the sight of them Frances begged the man not to take her away, because she had to take care of her little babies. The man looked at her with great sympathy and said OK. With that, Frances woke up.

The doctors told her that she nearly died and they couldn't explain why she had not. They hadn't found the source of the bleeding and were still trying to deal with it when all of a sudden the bleeding stopped and her vitals returned to normal. It was all very unexplained and mysterious.

Unfortunately, as time went on Frances and Richard began to have problems in their marriage. That was a really tough time for Frances, and that's her story to tell. But what I can say is that at just twenty-one, she seemed to have the weight of the world on her shoulders and life was very difficult for her.

Eventually, when Aoife was two and Eoghan was five, Frances and Richard split up. Gathering up a small bag of belongings from their flat on Charlemont Street, she came to live with Joe, Conor and me. She stayed with us for a few months before she found her own place, a little flat in Rialto.

I think it was around this time alcohol became a crutch for Frances. A young single mother with two kids, and very little money, she found it difficult to cope. She was also very lonely and her self-confidence was at rock bottom. I was never aware of how bad Frances's drinking got; she hid it from me well as she knew I wouldn't approve. Life went on like that for a while for Frances and

I don't think it was until she met Brian Allen that things started to turn around for her.

Brian was a lovely guy from Cork. He came into her life and loved her and her kids with all his heart. He encouraged her with her music too, and became her manager, taking care of the business side of things. I think with Brian by her side her confidence began to grow. She started singing with a traditional band called Arcady and built up a following for herself.

A few years after she met Brian she came down to Conor and Danny's sports day with Eoghan and Aoife to cheer on the boys. My daughter Róisín was only about six months old then. Our families were, and still are, extremely close; our kids grew up side by side and because of this they have a special bond. I remember I won a bottle of wine that day in the raffle and I gave it to her, thinking little of it. She told me afterwards that that bottle of wine was the last drink she ever had.

When Frances's musical career started to take off I was so happy for her. She often came and asked me for advice in those early years and I was always happy to give it, and I encouraged her in any way I could. I know it must have been difficult for her to come into the industry; there was always the risk that people would make comparisons between us. But Frances developed her own style and her own niche and she created a very successful solo career.

On top of all her family and music commitments, in the mid-2000s, Frances went back to college for two years to train as an addiction counsellor. Despite having left school at fifteen with few qualifications, she worked really hard and graduated from college. She then went on to do further training in the Rutland Centre.

Through this training and her own experiences Frances realized that more support was needed for family members, who were often extremely anxious and worried about their loved ones who suffered from addiction. So, in 2009 she set up the RISE foundation (Recovery In a Safe Environment), supporting family members of the addicted in their feeling of powerlessness, heartache, stress and anxiety. I have never seen her more fulfilled in her work or more dedicated to the people she tries to help and the cause of the RISE foundation.

After such a tough start Frances completely turned her life around; she followed her love of music and then pursued her need to help others. At the same time, she managed to raise two beautiful, happy kids.

Frances is such a caring person and when we're together I have a banter and a connection with her that I have with no one else. She will always tell you that I have her in stitches of laughter because, for some reason, she finds me very funny. The truth is, it makes me so happy to make her laugh. I think growing up she always looked up to me, but I can honestly say that now I look up to her. That wild teenager has turned into a great woman – and I am so proud of her.

6

All the world shall be of one religion

MY SECOND-CLASS teacher was called Miss Shaw. She was strict, like all the teachers back then, but she wasn't cruel. I had just spent the last three years under the tyranny of Sister Norbert so it was a welcome change moving into Miss Shaw's classroom. She was a young teacher, in her thirties with dark hair, and I remember she had these big pointy boobs that sort of stood out. One day a classmate told me the reason she had those big boobs was because she was expecting twins. I then thought that that meant there was a baby in each boob.

One day Miss Shaw was teaching us a song and got us all to stand beside the piano and sing with her. She stopped in the middle of the song and turned and pointed at me. 'Are you in the choir?' she asked. I told her I wasn't and she told me, 'Well, you should be.'

The next day Sister Herman, who ran the choir, came

into the classroom and asked me to come outside. She took me to the music room where there was a piano and asked me to sing a song. My father had taught me an old ballad called 'Beautiful Bundoran' so that was what I sang for her.

> *Beautiful Bundoran by the silvery sea*
> *Where golden strands*
> *Charm so grand*
> *Ever calling me*

I wasn't nervous. I suppose it was because of my dad's hoolies. He would often bring friends home from the pub on a Sunday for the holy hour and they'd spend the afternoon playing tunes and singing songs in our house. Mammy would make them soup and sandwiches and the men all drank Guinness. Everyone would have a party piece, children included, and we would perform in front of the assembled gang. So I suppose that day when Sister Herman asked me to sing it wasn't strange for me to perform at the piano because adults were often asking me to sing.

I must have impressed her because when she finished she said, 'You have a very strong voice, Mary. I want you to join the choir.' I was delighted; I had never been picked for something so important before.

St Louis Primary School's choir was called 'The

Young Dublin Singers' and was made up of about fifty girls, aged eight to twelve. It was a well-known and well-respected choir in Dublin. They had won competitions, sang at special masses, weddings and funerals, and even did some TV shows on RTÉ.

When I went home that day and told Mammy the good news she was over the moon. She knew how hard it was to get into the choir and it was quite uncommon for a student from second class to be asked to join; it was usually the more senior girls that got in. She was so proud of me she even gave me a kiss, which was something she didn't do very often.

Being in the choir involved rehearsing through lunch on a Tuesday and coming in every Saturday morning from nine o'clock until one. Sometimes we would be taken out of class to rehearse if there was a big concert coming up. It was a three-part harmony choir and I was put in the seconds. I absolutely loved it.

Sister Herman taught me so much about harmony and how different notes can blend together to make a beautiful sound. I used to look forward to every single rehearsal, even those held on Saturday mornings; hearing all those voices singing in harmony together was magical and made me feel good inside.

Proinsias Ó Ceallaigh was our main conductor for our performances, but it was Sister Herman who did all the hard work. She would teach us all the parts and drill them into us before Mr Ó Ceallaigh even got into the room with us. She was as tough as nails and was prone to digging her bony knuckles into your arm or shoulder if she heard you sing the wrong words or, heaven forbid, sing out of tune. But despite, or because of, her terror tactics, she got the best out of us and worked very hard to get us ready for Mr Ó Ceallaigh. Little did I think that those early years in St Louis choir were to lay the foundation of a future career.

About three years after I joined the choir, all the classes were called to the assembly. I remember my class was walking two by two along the corridors and up ahead I saw Sister Herman. She was picking out girls from each class as they walked by. I saw the girls she was picking out and noticed they were all choirgirls. As I walked by I sort of expected her to call my name but her eyes met mine for a few seconds then she just turned away. This confused me because some of the girls she picked out were weaker singers than me. I instinctively knew there was something big happening and I wasn't going to be part of it.

It turned out that Bing Crosby was coming to Dublin to perform a show for St Patrick's Day, which was to be televised in Ireland and shown all over America. A selection of The Young Dublin Singers would be singing with him for the event.

I was gutted that I wasn't picked. I told my mammy

and I could tell she was disappointed too, but she still gave me a smile and said, 'Ah well, there'll be other times for you, Mary.'

The situation frustrated me. I was never big-headed but I knew I was a good singer and even after that rejection I didn't doubt my own ability. I just didn't understand why I wasn't picked.

I realized, as I got a little older, that the nuns in St Louis were impressed by where you came from, who your parents were and, when it came to big occasions such as this, how well dressed you were, rather than how good a singer you were. I was from Charlemont Street – not perceived to be the best part of town. We had no running hot water, no shower or bath; we washed once a week in a tin tub in front of the fire, and Mammy had to boil water before she washed all our clothes by hand. Of course, my parents could only afford one uniform for me, so after years of washing and wearing I'm sure my clothes looked shabby next to many of the other girls.

The girls Sister Herman picked that day were well groomed; they had shiny hair, done up in ringlets, pristine white shirts and freshly pressed, pleated gym-slips. Those were the girls she wanted to represent her choir, regardless of whether they were the best singers or not. When the entire choir was involved in a concert, I was never put in the front row; my uniform was always hidden behind someone else's.

Despite this setback, Sister Herman made me leader of the seconds the following year when I was in sixth class.

One day around that time, Sister Herman brought in a 'special visitor' to the school; I think it was an inspector, or a 'cigire' as they were known in Irish, and she really wanted to impress him. She brought this man into the choir rehearsal and after we sang a song for him she got us to stand up while she introduced us all by name.

When it came to me I saw embarrassment flash across her face before she said, 'Mary Blake.' I looked at her surprised. I was leader of the seconds, I had been in her choir for years, and she knew my name wasn't Blake. It really annoyed and puzzled me; why couldn't she say my name? Was there something wrong with the word Black?

I was amazed that she could do such a thing and, as I was only twelve at the time, it made me more self-conscious than ever of my name. I'd already developed a bit of a hang-up about it because once some of the rougher kids around my area knew my name was Black, they'd call me 'nigger'. It didn't help that I had dark hair and sallow skin.

I guess if there was a positive to be had from all of this, the seeds of sympathy and compassion for those who had to endure discrimination were planted in my mind at a young age and today, looking back, I can only imagine how hard it must have been for black people to grow up in Ireland in the 1960s when this nun couldn't even say the word.

It was at this stage that I also became more aware of class discrimination and the abuse meted out to youngsters by certain Catholic religious orders. They taught the children of my generation through fear.

There was little positivity or happiness in the class-room, particularly for a girl like me from Charlemont Street – someone from the lower end of the social spectrum.

I think I also realized that though corporal punish-ment was an accepted part of the education system in St Louis, it was nothing compared to what my brothers and many other children experienced at the hands of the Christian Brothers throughout Ireland.

For my part, I can genuinely say that through the narrow-mindedness of many of the nuns who taught me, who only saw me as a 'common' child, I was left lacking any real sense of self-worth. I may have brazened things out on the surface, and I could act confidently when I needed to, but deep down I had some doubts and insecurities, all born out of a sense of not being quite good enough to compete with those who came from more affluent backgrounds. And although this might seem minor compared to the beatings and other abuse children endured during this era, it certainly left its mark on me and affected me as a child, and as an adult.

Having said that, the St Louis nuns were not the worst religious order out there – they did educate well and had a passion for singing and music from which I benefited greatly.

7

Oh, what you wouldn't give to be down on that pier once again

WHEN IT WAS time for me to leave St Louis Primary School, a little bit of luck came my way in the form of free education. Throughout my time in primary school I had always accepted that I wouldn't be going on to St Louis Secondary School, like many of my classmates, as it was a private school with high fees. I would most likely be going on to Rathmines Technical College or another public school like most of the girls from my area.

It just so happened that the year I left St Louis Primary School was the year St Louis Secondary School went public. This was a great opportunity for me to get a good second-level education free of charge – and, as a plus, I got to stay with the close friends I had made in school, like Marie Fennell, Nuala McGlynn and Denise Cassidy.

While the fees were waived, the traditions of the school remained the same, and the cost of kitting me out was likely to be a problem. We had to have two sets of uniforms, indoor and outdoor shoes, a gabardine coat, a blazer, a beret and a PE uniform on top of all the new books. From the outset my mother was really worried about all the expense and told me, 'You're going to have to get a job to help pay for all this.'

My best friend Olive Elliot who lived across the road in Charlemont Street found herself in a similar position to me at that time. She had just finished primary school and was planning on going to St Anne's in Milltown, which had just been made public. So, in June of 1968, the two of us set about finding a job for the summer. You had to be fourteen to work legally at the time, so we knew we'd have to lie our way into any job we went after; Olive was twelve and I had just turned thirteen. We heard about this little factory off Synge Street that made Lucky Bags and decided to chance our arm with the boss there.

When we went in to see the man in charge he took one look at Olive and said, 'You're not fourteen.' He gave me a quick once-over and asked, 'What age are you?'

I answered as quickly and as confidently as I could, 'Fourteen!'

I got the job. The hours would be from nine in the morning until six, Monday to Friday, with an hour for lunch. I was paid £2.50 a week. There was also a system called 'piece work', which meant you could get paid more depending on how fast you worked.

For those of you who are unfamiliar with Lucky Bags, let me explain. They were colourful paper bags filled with three or four little trinkets and sweets and were made for children to buy in shops. There were boys' ones and girls' ones that were usually differentiated by the colour of the bag and, of course, its contents. A boy's bag might contain a toy soldier or a scary spider along with a sweet or two, while a girl's bag might have a plastic spinning top or toy umbrella alongside her sweets.

In the factory everyone filled their own bags; it wasn't a regular production line. Every day I'd sit down at my station, where I'd be given a box of each item to go into the bags provided. After a while I got very fast at it, which was a good thing because that's when the 'piece work' would kick in. The more boxes of goodies you got through, the more money you'd make, so you had to be very fast.

There was one girl who would get through her boxes incredibly fast and was much quicker than everyone else. She was a bit older than me and because she was so quick I thought that she was just really good at her job. She'd always have a bigger paycheck at the end of the week than anyone else.

One morning I noticed the boss standing over at her boxes of made-up Lucky Bags. He seemed to be feeling the insides of the bags. Next thing, he opened a few of them and poured the contents on to the table in front of her. There were three or four of every toy in each bag and I'll never forget how shocked I was. Not only was she giving away his merchandise, but she was getting him to pay her more for doing so.

Although she was cheating, I thought it was very clever of her to get away with it for so long. At the age of thirteen, it wasn't something that I'd ever thought of doing, and I was glad I didn't, because she was sacked on the spot. It caused quite a stir when she stood up from the table as proud as punch, told the boss to 'Fuck off and keep your manky job', then walked out.

I worked all of June and July that summer and every Friday I'd run home with my wages to Mammy. I'd hand it over and she'd give me back a few shillings as pocket money.

I didn't really like working in the Lucky Bag factory; it was a monotonous job and for a thirteen-year-old working eight hours a day seemed like a lifetime. In fact, during that whole summer I looked forward to the first two weeks of August, when all the factories and work places closed down and I'd be able to go up to Rathlin.

I had spent every summer of my childhood on Rathlin Island. The five of us and Mammy would usually head up in early July and my father would join us when he got off work at the start of August.

Rathlin was a magical place. It was exciting for us as inner-city kids to be lifted out of the busy streets of Dublin to this wonderfully rural island that my father came from. To have the freedom to run wild in the fields and to help Auntie Mary and Uncle Michael on the family farm was such a complete contrast to our life in the city and I loved it.

Part of the excitement of the trip was the journey there. We didn't have a car so we'd take the train from Dublin to Belfast, then another train from Belfast to Ballymena, then a bus from Ballymena to Ballycastle. In Ballycastle Mammy would always treat us to fish and chips on the pier while we waited for the little boat that would take us across to the island. Us kids loved the boat ride. The seas could be very rough on that stretch but to us it was like a roller-coaster. The bigger the waves the better . . . no fear.

My mother, however, looked terrified during most of this particular part of the journey; she would be green in the face with fear and more times than not she could be found clinging for dear life to a post in the middle of the boat, praying in hushed tones that got louder as the waves got higher: 'Sacred Heart of Jesus, I place all my trust in thee.'

Rathlin at one time had a population of over a thousand people. But with the famine in the 1800s and the emigration of younger people like my father and his siblings, as the years went on there were only about a hundred people left living there. While it lies six miles off the Antrim coast, it is only fifteen miles from the Mull of Kintyre on the coast of Scotland. As a result, the island was heavily influenced by Scottish music and dance, and my father learnt quite a few Scottish tunes growing up there.

Without really realizing it, it seems I have gathered a large collection of Scottish songs throughout my career. Songs like 'Bogey's Bonnie Bell', 'Rarie's Hill', 'Anachie Gordon', 'Will Ye Gang' and 'Turning Away' were the songs that really spoke to me and I always enjoyed performing them. I would never choose a song just because of what country it came from, but as I look back at the songs I've recorded over the years, it seems like I am drawn to ones from Scotland. I think growing up around my father and his family, playing Scottish tunes and songs, ingrained in me a certain comfort and security with the style that I never lost.

That summer in 1968 I only had two precious weeks on Rathlin, and as always I stayed in Glacklugh on the Black family farm. It was nestled on the upper end of the island with a beautiful view of Ballycastle and the cliffs along Fairhead.

The running of the farm had been left in the hands of Daddy's brother and sister, Uncle Michael and Auntie

Mary, after their mother died. They mostly farmed cows and sheep on those thirty-five acres and kept a few hens too. After helping out in the morning us kids would spend our days exploring the coastline attached to the farm called the O'Beirne; there you'd see fat seals perched on the rocks off the shore and find caves and rock pools – all waiting to be discovered.

Being on Rathlin was when I felt most happy back then. It was the best part of my childhood. In those surroundings we could all be children in the most innocent sense of the word. Without a worry or a care. But soon the responsibilities I had left behind in Dublin crept up on me.

The weeks flew by and in the middle of August I had to go back to Dublin. I begged my mother to let me stay. The rest of the family were staying in Rathlin for another two weeks and I couldn't bear the thought of going back to work in the factory.

I pleaded with my mother before we got on the boat back to Ballycastle: 'Please, Mam, I don't want to go back to Dublin; please let me stay for these last two weeks before I go back to school.'

But she wouldn't budge. 'No, Mary, you have to go back. I just can't manage it without you.'

I knew my wages helped in the house but in my thirteen-year-old head I was bitter. I had already worked for two months and made more than enough to pay for what I needed to start school; I thought I deserved those last two weeks of fun and freedom. But I got on the boat with my mother anyway, who would be staying in Dublin with me while I was working. I'm sure it hurt her as much as it did me to not let me stay, but I know now she had no other choice. She needed the income.

As we pulled away from the harbour and waved goodbye to my brothers and sister standing on the pier I felt the tears of anger and longing well up. Anger at my mother for making me leave, longing to stay with my siblings on this beautiful island. In that moment I got a glimpse of the pain my father must have felt when he took that same journey thirty-five years before, although when he left he was leaving his family and home for good.

My father, Kevin Black, was born in December 1907. It was a particularly harsh winter that year, which meant it was too dangerous for his family to make the journey across to Ballycastle to register his birth. He wasn't registered until the twelfth of July, 1908, and that's the date he always celebrated his birthday. I don't think he even knew exactly when he was born.

Daddy was third youngest of eight children of James and Teresa Black: Michael, Katie, Mary, Maggie, James, Kevin, John, Tessie.

When Daddy was six years old his father died of a

heart attack at just fifty and my grandma was left to raise the young family on her own in Glacklugh. Although times were tough, the family was pretty self-sufficient on the farm and lived off the land. However, when each child came of age they knew they'd have to go to the mainland or abroad to find work. There wasn't enough to sustain them on the island, and one by one they all left.

When it came Daddy's time to leave, an uncle who lived in New Zealand sent him a one-way ticket to join him there. Daddy thought about it, but Grandma begged him not to go. She knew if he went so far she'd never see him again. So, instead of travelling to the other side of the world he stayed put, and when he was in his early twenties he took up an apprenticeship as a plasterer with a builder in Cushendun. He jumped at the chance to learn a new skill, and although it was a wrench to leave the island, this job meant he could stay fairly close to home. He learnt quickly and got on well with his boss.

Every Sunday morning he'd cycle the fifteen miles from Cushendun to Ballycastle. Back then there wasn't even one boat a day; there was no such thing as a day trip to Rathlin. You might be able to go over one morning and come back the next but the water was so rough on that stretch of sea there was always the risk that the little open-top boats that took you across might not be able to get back. If it was bad there was a chance you could be stuck on the island for weeks. And so my father would sit on the pier in Ballycastle smoking his untipped Player's cigarettes and gaze across at Rathlin. This little routine gave him solace, and soothed the homesickness he felt.

Music, too, was a medium through which he escaped his longing for home. Shortly after moving to Cushendun he started up the Kevin Black Ceili Band with some friends he'd made. The music he played with the band was the music he grew up with on Rathlin. On the island, Protestants and Catholics lived side by side and mixed socially. The music my father learnt reflected this. He would play a medley of tunes that might include the air of 'A Nation Once Again' and then, 'The Sash My Father Wore'. They were tunes that echoed the Catholic/Protestant divide and in a way expressed the political differences that were prevalent in the six counties. But to him they were just tunes; it was just music. Growing up on Rathlin he was a little naïve and certainly wasn't aware of all the trouble that was bubbling under the surface on mainland Northern Ireland.

One day his boss called him to the office.

'Kevin,' he said sadly, 'I'm going to have to let you go. You're a great worker and I'm very fond of you, but there have been reports that you're playing rebel tunes at night. There's nothing I can do, it's out of my hands.' His boss was a good Protestant man and felt bad about the decision he had to make. He told my father he was blacklisted in every police barracks in the six counties as they thought he was a rebel promoting the Catholic cause and he'd never get plastering work in the North again. Daddy was bewildered. He learnt the true nature of what was going on in the North the hard way. Protestants ruled and he had no choice but to head south.

In 1935 Daddy arrived in Dublin knowing no one. From the train station he jumped on the first bus that came by, the number 20, whose conductor pointed him towards Charlemont Street, and who also gave him the address of a Mrs Roche who was known to provide room and board.

She was a great woman who looked after him well. Coincidentally, she also turned out to be the great-grandmother of my best friend Olive who I grew up with. Daddy stayed in digs there for thirteen years, right up until the day he married my mother.

My father loved Dublin, where he lived out the rest of his life, and he always had a lot of time for Dublin people; they'd made him welcome and showed great kindness to him throughout the years. Despite this, Rathlin was never far from his thoughts and he lived for those two weeks every summer, relishing the prospect of going home. The island remained close to his heart to the day he died.

Daddy instilled in us a sense of place and heritage through his love for Rathlin Island. Though my siblings and I will always be proud Dubliners born and bred, that strong bond with our father's birthplace carried through our generation and into the next. My mother used to tell me that I was conceived on Rathlin and was a real 'Rathliner' by nature. I had inherited the Rathlin look, with dark hair and light eyes. While these days I don't make it up there as often as I'd like, when I do set foot on the island there's an instant feeling of belonging. Seeing my own children and my nieces and nephews in the old farmhouse on Glacklugh fills me with great joy. The love my father had for Rathlin lives on through them.

8

An open door was to a girl like the stars are to the sky

WHEN IT CAME to my secondary-school uniform my mother was determined not to let the side down. With the money I had made over the summer as well as some of her own she bought every single item on the uniform list brand new, and two sizes too big so I could grow into them. I looked like a right eejit on my first day with my gabardine coat down to my ankles and my red beret on my head, proud as punch. No one wore that beret at school, except a few of the extra studious types and me on that first day. After that it was cast aside and never seen again. Within a few weeks I had talked my mother into turning up the hem of my gabardine and my gym-slip to above my knee. Neither of them was ever taken down again, so by the time I reached fifth year it was like a mini skirt. And that's the way I wanted it.

I loved secondary school. I thought having a separate teacher for every subject was brilliant. If you didn't like your teacher you'd only have to wait forty-five minutes to go on to your next one. There was a freedom about it. I continued singing in the choir too, which was my favourite part of school.

At about the end of the first year I was asked by Sister Herman to go down to Jury's Hotel on Dame Street; they wanted some of The Young Dublin Singers to take part in their Summer Irish Cabaret, and I was to be one of them. It was a long-running show and was very popular with tourists. Hal Roche was the MC, and Austin Gaffney played the lead role. They fitted me out in an Irish Cailín costume: a green silk midi skirt with full petticoats underneath, a white shirt with a big collar and puff sleeves and a black-velvet waistcoat with gold buttons. It was similar to what you would imagine a glamorous female leprechaun might wear.

We spent weeks rehearsing our parts, which consisted of singing and dancing in the chorus line. This was all new and exciting to me. The show ran seven nights a week. There were two troupes of Young Dublin Singers who would alternate each week. We were paid £7 per week, which was a fortune to me back then.

One of the things I had to do that was new to me was wear a bra. I was quite well developed for my age but was still a kid really and was embarrassed to wear one. On the long summer evenings when I'd be out playing with my friends my mother would call me into the house to get ready for the show that night. I'd have a wash and get dressed and reluctantly put on the bra. I would always be terrified that I'd meet someone on the way to Jury's and they'd notice I was wearing it. I was already self-conscious of my bust and felt the bra only made it stick out even more.

However, this was the only thing I didn't like about being a part of the show. I had great fun performing with the other girls every night. I stayed as part of the chorus line for two more summers. The money was a big plus too, especially in comparison to the Lucky Bag factory, which I was thrilled not to have to return to that summer.

Those summers with the Irish Cabaret taught me a lot about stage performance and the professional side of show business. Even though the music wasn't the style I would have chosen for myself, it was still a priceless experience and sowed the seed for my love of being on stage.

As I got older the music sessions at home became more frequent; Shay and Michael were getting older too and would bring musician friends home most weekends. By the time I was fifteen Shay had moved to a place in Prince Arthur Terrace in Rathmines. I would often go down to his little flat as there were regular sessions at the weekend there too. We'd sit around and the lads would play tunes and people would sing. It was exciting for me at that age to go up to Shay's flat. I got to hang out and sing in front of all his and Michael's friends. I was always allowed to stay out a little later because my brothers were there to look out for me and there was music involved too.

About that time Shay, Michael and myself decided to form a trad-folk band with two friends of theirs, Pascal Birmingham and John White, on mandolin and guitar. We called ourselves Terras, after the name of the road where Shay lived and where the sessions began, though we 'cleverly' changed the spelling to look cooler and sound more Irish. Back then there were quite a few folk clubs in and around Dublin where you could put your name down in an open-mic style, and get up and sing a few songs. We often played the Leinster Cricket Club in Rathmines, the Coffee Kitchen in town and the Web in Templeogue.

It was really more for fun than anything else. We decided to enter the Kilkenny Folk Festival competition. All our friends wanted to come and support us on the day so we hired a big bus and all travelled down to Kilkenny for the gig. Everyone was set for a great day out.

We were last on stage and had to sit through everyone else's performance beforehand. In that time the lads were getting more and more nervous and probably had a few too many drinks. By the time they got on stage they weren't exactly sober.

The plan was for Michael to start the song with a little tune on the banjo. But when he stood up to the mic and started playing, he was in the wrong key. We all just stood looking at each other in horror, until he realized his mistake. It threw us completely and our performance was pretty dismal. Even though we weren't great, all our loyal friends cheered enthusiastically as we dashed off the stage in embarrassment at the end of the set. We came nowhere, not that that was unexpected after such a performance.

The whole experience made me realize that this performing business wasn't as easy as it looked. Singing at a session was one thing, but getting up on a stage and singing into a microphone was totally different; it had to be taken seriously. My nerves had got the better of me and I realized I had a lot to learn. It was a joy for me to sing at a session but getting up in front of those bigger audiences started to become frightening. This was a fear that was to take a serious hold of me during the early years of my career.

Things fizzled out with Terras not too long after that poor performance. Shay got a job in Castlebar in Co. Mayo and the rest of us never kept it up when he left. It didn't bother me though; at sixteen I was beginning to discover other appealing hobbies outside of music.

Around that time Olive and I got friendly with a gang in

Ranelagh. Olive knew most of the girls as they went to her school in Milltown. The boys in the group were all guys about two years older than us from Sandymount and Mount Merrion, and most of them had motorbikes and the accompanying leather jackets and long hair. This was the coolest thing we had ever encountered and before long we both had boyfriends. Olive's was called Sully and mine was Cully. Sully was really handsome; he had a big build, blond hair and sparkling blue eyes. Cully was more slender, with dark curly hair and a beard. He was quieter and more mysterious than the other boys, which was something I liked about him.

In the summer of 1972 I turned seventeen. We'd finished school in early June and the holidays stretched out before us beautifully. With my best friend, our two gorgeous boyfriends and their Honda 175 and Yamaha 125 it looked like it was going to be the best summer yet. However, when our mothers got wind that Olive and I were hanging out with fellas with motorbikes we were forbidden to get on the back of them. Of course, that didn't stop us.

We rode around all summer on those motorbikes and even rode down to Courtown in Wexford one weekend. We never wore helmets either. For one thing it wasn't cool and for another, I loved too much the way my hair looked so curly after blowing in the wind for that long.

During the week we would have to be home by half ten. The boys would drop us home but only as far as the canal, as Olive's mother would usually have her head sticking out the window waiting to catch her on the back of the bike. We'd get off the bikes on Charlemont Street Bridge, have a lengthy snog goodbye and then walk the rest of the way home.

One night towards the end of the summer we left Ranelagh as usual to be home on time. Cully was a speed freak, so we got to the canal first and hung around for Sully and Olive to arrive. We waited for about half an hour but there was still no sign of them. We thought that maybe they had met someone on the street and stopped to talk, or perhaps they'd gone to the chipper, or something. By then I was anxious about the time and as I didn't want to get in trouble with Mam, I said goodbye to Cully and went on home.

Early the next morning my mother woke me with the words, 'Olive was in a terrible accident last night.'

I was in absolute shock and immediately a huge wave of guilt fell over me. Why didn't I wait longer? Why didn't we go back to look for them? Even though I had no idea about the accident, somehow I felt I'd abandoned her.

Apparently, after the four of us left Ranelagh that night, Sully and Olive stopped at some lights behind us. When the lights changed Sully pulled off at speed. Olive had been wearing a long knitted scarf that flew behind her on the motorbike and as they pulled away it got caught in the back wheel, yanking her off the back seat and dragging her behind the bike for several yards by the throat. Luckily the scarf snapped before it choked her. She received over forty stitches to her face and head and numerous cuts and bruises to the body as well as a severely bruised neck.

I was really upset when I heard the terrible news and had to see her. So I made my way over to James's Hospital where they told me she wasn't allowed any visitors. I sat in the reception area crying all day. I remember I had a woolly hat in my pocket and I started using it as a handkerchief. Later that evening I think the nurses took pity on me and they allowed me in to see Olive.

I was horrified. I could hardly recognize my best friend. Her face was swollen with stitches and bandages all over her, and her neck was black with bruises.

I burst into tears at the sight of her. 'I'm so sorry, Olive!' I blubbered. 'I'm so sorry I didn't wait for you.' I had never felt so guilty in my life. I should have made sure she was OK when she didn't arrive on the bridge; we were supposed to look out for each other.

She looked at me through swollen eyes, her head only slightly risen from the bed with a few pillows. 'I'm all right, don't worry,' she whispered.

But I desperately wanted her to know how sorry and upset I was so I handed her my soggy hat and said, 'Feel that, I haven't stopped crying all day.' To show her just how much I wrung it out till a drop fell on the bed.

She cracked a smile and said, 'I'm the one who had the accident!'

Olive was in hospital for about two weeks and although I'd like to say we never got on the motorbikes again, I can't; what I can say is that we wore helmets after that. It was a lesson learned and even the boys were generally more cautious following this horrible accident.

After a while our relationships with the boys ran their course. Things were getting a bit too deep and heavy with Cully so I told him I thought we should call it a day. I was young and didn't want to get tied down to anyone. I knew he was upset about it, but I didn't expect his reaction the following weekend.

On the following Saturday night me and all the girls headed off to Belfield where a huge disco was set up over two floors on the UCD campus. It was a very popular venue at the time with our age group, even though you were supposed to be over eighteen and attending the college to get in. We had fake IDs, of course.

Early in the night one of the girls came up to me on the dance floor and said, 'Mary, Cully's outside, he's really drunk and the bouncers won't let him in.' I brushed off the comment. He wasn't my problem; I wasn't his girlfriend any more and I certainly wasn't going out to him.

The next thing I know people were shouting and pointing at the window. When I went to see what all the commotion was about I could see Cully standing on the tiny ledge outside the window, banging on the glass and shouting my name. We were on the second floor! Apparently, after being rejected by the bouncers, he had crawled up the side of the building and, peering through the window, tried to search for me. I was shocked, and as our eyes met he lost his footing and fell forty feet to the ground below. Luckily, he fell on grass, although he did bump his head quite badly and broke his arm in the process. The bouncers ran out and carried him inside.

While waiting for the ambulance to arrive the bouncers tried to get him to lie down but Cully refused and just kept shouting my name. 'Mary! I want to talk to Mary. Mary Black!' Eventually I went down to him. A huge crowd had gathered by this time and when he saw me his face lit up and he said, 'Mary! I have a present for ya!' He handed me a box. Inside was a sterling silver bracelet. As I opened the gift he pleaded, 'I need to talk to you, Mary. Can we talk?'

I felt bad then, and I told him we could talk. I said I'd meet him next week in town. The ambulance arrived and I said goodbye. I didn't feel that bad, though. I turned around and went back up to the dance floor as the ambulance drove away.

I met him the next week and gave him back the bracelet. I think he knew then that it was properly over. He was a lovely guy but I was just too young and enjoyed being free. I suppose I was just like any teenager at that age. I loved music but also liked hanging out with boys and going to discos and wearing hot pants.

9

'The Loving Time'

LATER THAT YEAR one of my best friends, Marie, told me she really fancied this guy Joe O'Reilly. She used to see him studying in Rathmines library and thought he was gorgeous. She'd drag me in under the pretence that we were studying so she could check him out. I didn't see what she was getting so excited about. He was nice-looking but he didn't blow me away, to be honest.

Joe wasn't completely unknown to me; we had mutual friends at Synge Street School where he and my brothers went. I knew, too, that his family was in the music business. I suppose I knew by osmosis, I don't remember being told, but people knew he worked in Dolphin Discs and his father, Joseph Snr (J.P.), owned the chain of stores around Dublin.

I would often chat to his older brother Ger who was very friendly and had a bubbly personality. Joe was quieter. He had a West Coast look. He had long curly red hair and usually wore a Fair Isle sleeveless jumper, a check shirt, baggy jeans, desert boots – and he always wore his John Lennon glasses. He had a real Californian Crosby, Stills and Nash look about him.

Marie had a summer job in Cassidy's in George's Street and Joe sometimes worked in Dolphin Discs in Steven's Street around the corner. When I visited Marie at work she would say to me, 'Go round and see if Joe O'Reilly is working in Dolphin Discs there!'

So being the good friend that I was I'd go around to Joe's shop and ask for something really obscure and have a bit of a chat with him or Ger. Afterwards I'd run back to Marie and tell her, 'Yeah he's there, he's there!'

Joe played Gaelic football with a lot of lads I knew: Paul Dowling, Eugene McCarthy, Larry Crowe and Ciaran O'Farrell (who was going out with Olive).

There was a game planned that someone invited us to, out in Hollywood in Wicklow, so Marie and I decided to head along. I was going primarily to see some of our friends play, though, of course, Marie had already found out that Joe was going to be there too. And there would be a few pints to be had in a pub nearby after the match.

It was a clear, warm, summer's evening, a nice day for a game, though that's about all I can remember of the game itself. After having a few drinks in the bar across the road we heard there was a céilí on in the local hall, which we all barrelled over to, players and supporters alike.

The hall seemed to be packed with most of the population of Hollywood, which wasn't that many really, but they made us feel welcome. There was nothing fancy about it, it was just a basic gathering of locals having a dance to the tunes of the local accordion and fiddle players, but that suited us perfectly.

Before long we were up on the floor dancing and having a laugh.

We had no lift home, but we knew Joe had a car so I asked him if Marie and me could fob a lift back to Dublin later that night. He said sure, no problem.

But at about midnight, Joe decided he was going home. I was disgusted! We had only been there for about an hour and were having such a good time. I didn't want the night to end so soon.

We tried to get him to stay but Joe put his foot down and said, 'Look, do yous want a lift or not? I have work in the morning. I'm leaving now.'

We had no choice. There was no other way to get back to the city so we went with him. I was really pissed off. I remember scowling at him in the back of the car and telling him, 'Sure you're a right drip!' Needless to say neither of us talked to each other the whole way home. I was sulking for having to leave such a great night, and he was fuming because I wasn't grateful to him for the lift home. We certainly did not hit it off, that's for sure.

*   *   *

Later that summer, a friend from St Louis School, Moya Kearney, invited Marie and me down to Courtown, Co. Wexford for the weekend. She was going out with a friend of Joe's, named Ciaran O'Neill. Joe's father had a pub on the main street in Courtown and Joe and his friend would work there during the summer. In fact, there was a great gang of people who worked down there: some of Joe's family and the Knoxes, who were friends of Joe's, as well as a few other friends from Dublin. Maura and J.P. always welcomed friends of Joe and his siblings with open arms. They were very broad-minded parents for their time. They were only a little younger than my parents but to me it felt like there was almost a generation between them. They created a great environment down in Courtown, and there was always a holiday feeling about the place.

On the way down to Courtown Marie was trying to persuade me to fancy Sean Knox, one of Joe's best friends, which I went along with; he was a good-looking guy.

When we arrived there, there was an infectious buzz about the place. We were young and the summer was stretching out before us and everyone was on good form. By the end of the night Sean had spent most of the night chatting up Marie! She wasn't complaining and I thought it was hilarious how quickly she had jumped ship and switched her attention from Joe to Sean.

I clearly remember that that weekend was pretty full on. Dublin was playing Meath on the Sunday and there was a large gang of GAA fans, myself included, gearing up for the match. We were all passionate Dublin football supporters and headed off in a convoy of cars to Navan, where the match was being held. The stadiums back then were basic, with maybe a few terraces, not what you'd call stadiums these days. But this never bothered us or dampened our spirits. We were young and just wanted to be at the match.

There was a big crowd that day, and I'm happy to report Dublin beat Meath. They'd won the All-Ireland Final the previous year too, so the supporters were really out in their droves, wearing their blue team colours with pride.

I think our group of friends thought we had an extra connection to the 'Dubs' because one of the players, Anton O'Toole, was from our local club, Synge Street. Anton had made it on to the team the year before when they won the Sam Maguire Cup. Also our Synge Street Senior team coach was Donal Colfer and he was part of the Dublin management team with Kevin Heffernan. Anton would go on to win three more All-Ireland Championships with Dublin and a hat trick of All-Stars in 1975, 1976 and 1977.

After the match that day we stopped at a little pub in Enfield on the way home to celebrate. We were all having a great time, and I remember what happened next as clear as yesterday. Somebody said something funny and I started laughing; I looked up and across the table Joe was laughing too. Our eyes met and *bang!* I can't really explain it, it was just instant attraction from that moment on. Before that there was nothing. Something happened in that moment that flipped a switch in me. At the time I didn't know how Joe felt about me, but after that I saw him at one or two other outings, and I thought (and hoped) that maybe there was a spark of interest from him. I was never quite sure.

It was on one Thursday night, when my friend Olive and I were bored, that we decided to go down to our local pub, Cassidy's, on Camden Street for a Guinness and a smoke. We got to the pub, ordered our drinks and took a seat near the door. We chatted away about this and that – what was going on with our friends, and who liked who; it had been one of our staple conversation topics for the last few weeks. I had spent most of my free time since the Courtown trip thinking about the whole situation with Joe. I didn't know what, if anything, he felt about me. He never really gave me any indication that he liked me, not as far as I could see, but I hoped that I would meet him at a party or a game and we'd hit it off.

After a few minutes' talking, Olive stared over my shoulder and said, 'You'll never guess who's just after walking in the door!'

I went statue still. 'Who?' I asked.

'Sean Knox, Ciaran O'Brien and Joe O'Reilly.'

'Fuck off!' I answered. 'You're messin'!' This was a pub they never came into. They were from Templeogue.

'I swear to God, Mary!' she said, an excited smile on her lips.

I could hardly believe my luck, and was so happy to see Joe. Before long the three lads came over, sat down and had a pint with us. A few minutes later I jumped up and, making some excuse, went to the public phone in the corner of the bar. I dialled Marie's number and when she answered I whispered down the receiver, 'Marie, you'll never guess who just walked into Cassidy's! Sean Knox! You have to come down, I think he's here looking for you.'

Marie knew at that stage that I liked Joe but I honestly thought Sean wanted to see Marie and that's why the lads had come down to the pub; it was the only thing that made sense to me – and I certainly didn't think it had anything to do with me and Joe.

'Mary, I can't, I'm washing my hair!' Marie said. She had long black hair which reached down to her waist and washing it was a serious ordeal, so I knew she wasn't making excuses.

I went back to the table and Olive and I spent the rest of the night chatting to the three lads. When it was closing time and we were all getting up to leave, Joe pulled me aside and said, 'Mary, would you like to come to a twenty-first birthday party with me on Saturday?'

My heart jumped, but somehow I managed to keep things together and I answered him in the most casual tone possible, 'Yeah sure.'

'Great,' he said. 'I'll pick you up at eight.' Sean and Ciaran (who we called Noddy) were parked outside the pub waiting in Noddy's Morris Minor and Joe jumped in and waved me goodbye. The second the car went out of view I started doing cartwheels and danced down the street. I was so excited. When we got home me and Olive were still laughing and jumping around and my mother came down the stairs and asked, 'What's all the commotion about?'

I never used to talk to my mother about boyfriends or anything like that at that time, but I was so happy I blurted out, 'Oh, Mam! This gorgeous guy is after asking me out!'

She was thrilled for me but no one could have been more excited than I was.

Joe picked me up at eight o'clock sharp on Saturday night. I had spent most of that evening in my bedroom labouring over what to wear and trying to tame my frizzy black curls while a fourteen-year-old Frances occasionally whizzed in and out making kissing noises on the back of her hand. I was just about ready when my mother shouted up the stairs.

'Mary, Joe's here for you!'

My heart jumped a little and I took one last look in the mirror at the back of my wardrobe. I had decided to wear a grey spotted pinafore dress and had pinned my hair back, off my face. When I look back it was a horrendous outfit really, but I thought I looked lovely at the time.

After fixing a few stray hairs I rushed down the stairs and through Black's General Grocers. Joe was standing next to his beat-up white Renault 4 and opened the passenger door for me. I jumped in and we headed off to the party.

It was a little awkward to begin with, as first dates can be when you're young, but soon we both began to relax and have fun. It was the birthday of a friend of Joe's from college. They studied Commerce together at University College Dublin. I didn't know anyone at the party, it was all a bit strange to me this college scene, but I was having fun hanging out with Joe so I didn't mind.

The night flew by and all too soon Joe was driving me home. As I sat in the car with him outside my parents' house I sort of expected a peck on the cheek or to be asked when he could see me again, but neither came.

I was disappointed and felt awkward, so I just jumped out of the car and smiled a goodnight. Joe pulled away but as I was about to open my front door I heard a call from down the street. It was our friend Ciaran O'Farrell. He was stopping Joe to have a chat and Joe pulled in. He then spotted me outside my house and called me over too. We stood beside Joe's car and chatted for a while to each other and through the window to Joe. Eventually, Ciaran left and once again Joe and I were left to say an awkward goodbye.

But this time, before I could rush away uncomfortably, Joe blurted out, 'Do you want to hop in and say goodbye again?' As I sat back in the passenger seat of that old Renault 4 he leaned across and gave me a kiss and asked, 'Do you want to go out again sometime?'

I smiled in response. I suppose he felt just as awkward as I did on that first date.

I had only been going out with Joe for a few weeks or so when we went to Castlebar to visit some of my brother Shay's friends. Shay, John, Steve, Rory and Jerry were all great musicians. I often went over for visits to Castlebar, the sessions were always amazing and I loved spending time there. This time, though, Joe drove me down so it was the first time I didn't have to hitch a ride.

The atmosphere in the local pub, the Humbert Inn, was mighty that night. Joe was blown away by the music and the singing he was hearing. At the time I was singing

111

songs like 'Crazy Man Michael', 'Bogey's Bonnie Belle', a Scottish song of unrequited love and parental meddling, and 'Aonach Mhalla', an old lullaby I knew from my school days. The boys played tunes like 'The Lonesome Boatman', 'The Flogging Reel' and 'Napoleon's Retreat'.

After three nights of music in the Humbert, Joe turned around and said to all of us, 'I think you should record an album together, this stuff is really great!' As well as Dolphin Discs, Joe's father also owned an Irish record label called Dolphin Records. We were amazed and immediately jumped at the chance!

The following Friday we found ourselves sitting in a studio in Dublin staring at each other wondering what we would record. There was Shay Kavanagh (guitar), John Donegan (mandolin), Steve Dunford (bodhrán) and Rory Somers (uillean pipes). We had only ever played together at pub sessions and had no time to rehearse for the recording so we all jumped in and just did what we would do in the pub. There was an innocence about it. We sang and played from the heart.

The whole album was recorded and mixed in two days, rough and ready. It was a new experience for us; we were all a bit green but at the same time hugely excited at the prospect of bringing out an album. It was to be the first step on a long musical journey for me.

I often wonder what direction my career would have taken if I hadn't met Joe. He was hugely supportive in encouraging me to follow my musical path. He always believed in me, even when I didn't always believe in myself.

We named the band and the album General Humbert after the pub in Castlebar where it all began. Although it didn't become popular, there was a bit of notice taken of the album and an awareness of who we were on the music scene. With that awareness came some gigs and festivals in Dublin and around the country.

At the time the members of the band all had various jobs. John was in college in Trinity, I was a waitress in the Harcourt Hotel, Rory worked in the civil service, Steve was studying and Shay did a bit of playing in and around Castlebar. We loved playing together and we always had a great time, but we needed our jobs to earn a living, so it was never really a full-time thing.

10

I've got no more smiles to win you

I SPENT THE next year seeing Joe. It was a normal boyfriend/girlfriend relationship; we were into the same things – music, sport, hanging out with our friends. We'd go to gigs, sessions and games and most of our friends hung out in a group together so there was always craic at the weekend. We had a lot of fun and it was a very happy time in my life, being young and in love.

The following summer, in 1976, two friends of mine, Larry Crow and Eimear O'Carroll, were talking about going to Jersey for the summer and asked me if I would be interested in going. I knew I'd miss Joe but I was ready for something new, a bit of adventure. I left my waitressing job without a second thought. I knew I could pick up another when I got back.

We arrived in St Helier and were taken out to the Carnation Retreat Farm and shown where we were going to stay. This turned out to be a massive barn that was partitioned off in small rooms with two metal beds in each and a little two-ring cooker. As far as equipment and furniture was concerned, that was all there was, but the place was crammed with migrant workers from Portugal and other parts of Europe. In fact, it felt a little bit like a refugee camp.

We were told our day would start at seven in the morning, we'd get an hour for lunch and we'd finish at five in the evening. It was more work than we were expecting, but we'd made the trip and decided to give it a go, hoping we'd have some fun along the way.

From day one it was a very hard graft. The carnations were grown in open-top glasshouses so we worked in searing heat all day. When we picked the carnations there was always one of the local workers at the top of the line; he or she would set the pace and everyone had to keep up or they would be in big trouble. In fact, some people lost their jobs because they couldn't keep up the pace.

As soon as they were picked, the flowers were put into a cool room to be packed and sent off to the four corners of the globe. Larry got a job picking potatoes on another part of the island so it was just Eimear and me all summer. It was very hard work but we enjoyed it because we got to know a lot of the other foreign workers. They had very little English but somehow we all managed to communicate quite well.

Luckily, we had Saturday afternoons and Sundays off, so every weekend we'd meet up in St Helier with Larry and some of the friends he'd made. One Sunday, when I was particularly exhausted by the week's work, I took myself off to the beach. I was lying there on my own as Eimear wasn't really into sunbathing and had gone for a walk. I was in my new denim bikini, lying in front of the promenade, and I soon fell into a deep sleep. The next thing I was awoken with the shock of freezing cold water all around me! As I jumped up I could hear a huge round of applause from the promenade behind. A crowd had gathered to watch as the tide came in closer and closer to my sleeping form. Everyone stayed quiet until a wave crashed up around me and then the whole crowd started cheering and clapping. I was mortified, grabbed my stuff and ran from the beach.

In the middle of August, after two and a half months away, I felt homesick for my family and for Joe and I decided I wanted to go home. I told no one back home of my plans and got a flight back to Dublin and surprised them all. I walked into Black's General Grocers. Daddy happened to be behind the counter and I'll never forget the look on his face. He looked so happy to see me.

'Och, Mary, Mary, I'm delighted you're home!' In that moment I realized just from the expression on his face how much my dad loved me, although he never said it.

There was great excitement that I was home. Mammy put out a big dinner for us that night; we were all there, except Shay who was living in Liverpool at the time. It had been my first time ever away from home and I had missed all the familiar faces, the warmth that only a close family can provide, and I was so happy to be back.

Joe was in Courtown, where he was working for the summer, and I was keen to see him. I managed to get a lift down to Courtown from Noddy and Paul Dowling that weekend but, again, I kept it quiet. I didn't tell Joe I was coming to see him and, in fact, he had no idea I was home. I had bought a new pure white cotton gypsy top that hung off my shoulders, which I wore with jeans. My hair was plaited on both sides and clipped up to my head with little curls falling down. Having worked outside all summer, I was tanned and toned and looked the picture of health.

When we arrived, Paul jumped out of the car and, even though he knew it was supposed to be a surprise, when he ran into Joe he blurted out, 'You'll never guess who's outside! You'll never guess who's outside!' Paul just couldn't contain his excitement. To this day, although we're still friends and laugh about it now, I'll never forgive him for spoiling the big surprise. Of course, Joe was thrilled to see me home too, and there was another great homecoming in Courtown that night!

Like many young girls in Dublin at that time, I had started smoking at sixteen. I never really wanted to be a smoker, it was always more about fitting in with the crowd than enjoying the experience, and because of my passion for singing I knew I should stay well clear of cigarettes. A couple of weeks before Christmas that year Joe and I made a pact that we'd give up smoking together. We thought if we could get through all the Christmas socializing we could get through anything. It was the hardest thing I ever did but I got through it. I was determined and had psyched myself up not to slip.

But then one Sunday evening I met Joe for a quiet drink in the Barge. We were having a pleasant enough night until, out of nowhere, Joe said to me, 'I think we should split up. I think I'm too young for this and I'm just not ready for commitment.' I was in total shock. I sat in silence trying to take it in.

On the inside I was in bits. I was totally in love with Joe and his decision had come completely out of the blue for me. But I was proud; I didn't want him to see how upset I was, so I went along with it.

I said something like, 'Yeah, maybe you're right.' But I was in shock and I don't remember much about the conversation after that. I just went home and cried my eyes out.

Although my pride was hurt, I was very determined to stay off the cigarettes. I didn't want Joe to think that I was vulnerable and went back on them just because he'd broken up with me.

We kept in touch as friends after that. He'd call me now and then or we'd bump into each other when the gangs were out. Whenever I saw him I always pretended I was doing great. I never went back on the fags but Joe did, which I have to say made me feel a little better about myself. I found it hard seeing him, though. I sometimes would avoid certain places or parties because I knew he'd be there.

Years later, my sister Frances told me she used to feel so bad for me at the time. We shared a room and she could hear me crying myself to sleep every night. I was determined not to let anyone see I was upset and spent a lot of time out and about with my friends and singing when I could. But I suppose at night time, especially in the early days after the split, I let go a bit, never thinking Frances could hear me.

Life went on. I had a great group of friends and things were moving on with our band, General Humbert. I spent most of the following summer in Germany on tour with them doing festivals and gigs. I went on the odd date during that period with a few different guys, but no one really sparked my attention. I wasn't really interested, to be honest. I fancied the idea of being with someone but just didn't find anyone I liked enough to make the effort. Perhaps, too, I was still feeling a bit bruised and vulnerable.

Joe had gone to America that summer to travel and when he came back he called me. He told me he'd met someone, a cousin of a friend of his, and he was really keen on her. I pretended to be happy for him and began to accept that it was really over with Joe and me. I made a conscious decision to avoid seeing him, especially when he was with this other girl. I was told Joe would often ask after me on nights out, but Marie or Olive would make some excuse for me not being around, and would tell him I was fine.

On Stephen's Night that year I was out with the gang in the Synge Street club house having a few drinks and a sing song. Joe and the new girlfriend arrived in. Everyone was well on. At one point I went into the kitchen to get another drink and I walked in on Joe and his new girl. They were kissing and they didn't see me; I slipped out unnoticed. I was thoroughly fed up with the whole situation by then and was desperate to get away from it all.

I walked back into the main bar and said, 'Right, let's get out of here and go and see The Floating Dublin Blues Band out in Bray!' We knew a few of the lads in the band and thought we'd get a lift home off someone.

So, Marie, Caroline Kelly, Frances, Richard and I jumped on to a bus and headed out to Bray. We danced and drank the night away and had a great time. I put the episode of Joe and his new girlfriend behind me. It wasn't until the band told us they didn't have any room in the van to bring us home that things started to go downhill. There were no taxis, and, in fact, there were hardly any cars on the road because by then it was one o'clock in the morning.

It was a freezing night, and most of the girls weren't dressed for the weather, but there was nothing for it but to start the long walk home. And it was absolute torture. I remember Frances nearly crying, begging me to lend her my fur coat. But, to my shame, I was in no mood to share it, so I didn't give it to her; it was just too cold.

We walked about eight miles towards Dublin before a man stopped his car – a beautiful big Merc – and offered to give us a lift. Safety in numbers, so all six of us piled into the car and we were nearly kissing him in thanks.

After that night I made a conscious decision to try to let go of the whole Joe thing once and for all. I had seen him happy with his new girlfriend and, though that hurt, it made me realize that we were not meant to be together. As my mother often used to say, in fact I'm sure she said it to me then, 'What's for you won't go by you.'

I also became more determined than ever to move

forward and concentrate on my music. My heart had been broken but I had to get on with my life. That was my plan, but as things turned out, letting go was easier said than done.

11

'And the Larks They Sang Melodious at the Dawning of the Day'

Around that time I met a woman called Peggy Jordan. She lived in a big house on Kenilworth Square, Harold's Cross. She would come to sessions in Slattery's on Capel Street or Tailors' Hall where I'd be singing. Peggy loved traditional music and one day she approached me saying a film director had been in touch and had asked her to recommend a good Irish singer to sing on a feature-length film he was directing. The film was called *The Outsider* and it told the story of an American man whose grandfather had emigrated from Ireland to the States when he was in his twenties. The American became fascinated by his grandfather's story; he'd been caught up in the troubles and was a member of the IRA. The story takes him back to Ireland and his roots. The film score included Irish music and that was, as Peggy explained, where I came in.

The film company wanted to fly me over to Detroit for filming, which was strange because I didn't think I was going to actually be in the film, but I was more than happy to go along anyway. The night before I left for Detroit, I saw Joe and he asked me write to him, and I said I would. I noticed he had become more attentive that spring, even though we were still only friends, and proud as I was, I didn't let myself think about it too much – or get my hopes up that he'd had a change of heart.

The film organizers sent me my ticket and off I went on my own adventure. I felt very grown-up and independent. It was the first time I'd been to America and I was so excited. All I had when I arrived was my small suitcase and this guy's name from the film company: Chris Blackmore. It was only when I got to New York and had some time to think about things while waiting on my connection for Detroit that it occurred to me that this was all a bit risky. 'What the hell am I gonna do if this guy's not there?' I had no address, I knew nobody, I was a green 22-year-old. But I held my nerve and got on the plane anyway.

When I arrived in Detroit I got off the plane and went down to the baggage reclaim area, hoping against hope that someone would be there with a big sign saying 'Mary Black'. I suppose I was looking for someone who 'looked Irish'.

I looked around and noticed a guy who was dark, wore glasses and looked a bit odd, so I said to myself, 'It's definitely not him, anyway.' But slowly the passengers gathered their luggage and when there were only a couple of people left, I was beginning to get worried; there was only me and the guy with the glasses who looked 'a bit odd'. Turns out this was Chris Blackmore and he'd come to meet me.

Chris had been reluctant to approach me because I looked more Spanish than Irish – it had been a really hot May and I was as brown as a berry – and after introducing himself we got chatting and I realized he wasn't odd at all.

Chris drove me back to what looked like a really expensive hotel. My room had a huge bed, a private bathroom and it overlooked a courtyard and a massive swimming pool. I had never seen anything so posh, but I felt I could soon get used to the lifestyle!

On my first day I noticed there were caterers for the film crew and actors, and loads of people running around doing something for someone. The film seemed to have a huge budget, no expense was spared.

The next morning I was introduced to the director and various actors who were starring in the film. The actor Sterling Hayden played the grandfather and everyone was very nice and friendly. I loved the buzz and excitement, especially when I went out on location with the crew. The whole week was a fascinating experience. There was no mention of me being in any scenes but they certainly loved my singing. Every evening after the day's shooting the cast and crew would find somewhere to have a few drinks and a chat and someone would always ask me to sing. Back then it was all so easy. Someone would shout, 'Mary! Sing a song!' and I'd sing without hesitation, unaccompanied.

I had an amazing week on set, living in the lap of luxury, eating the best food and meeting famous people. This had been a totally different experience for me, and I loved it.

What a start to my summer. I got a cheque for $200 for my expenses, but as it turned out they didn't want to use me in the film, only to record my voice and put it in the movie later. They said they'd be in touch.

Although a little disappointed, I was hopeful that they would get back to me about the recording and I decided to make the most of my time in the States. I planned to head over to friends of mine, the Kings, who lived in Connecticut. They were originally from Curráin, Co. Mayo, and I met them during my trips to Castlebar. They had moved to America the previous year and had four young children. With a thriving business to run (Tom was a builder), they needed help to look after their kids. It was something I was happy to take on, although I have to admit that looking after the children was very hard work, and a bit of a reality check for me after my fantastic week of relative luxury in Detroit. I looked upon this as a different type of adventure and I managed to have some fun during my stay with the Kings.

After about four or five weeks in Connecticut, I jumped on a train and landed in New York's Grand Central Station, where I met up with Shay, Michael and Martin. Frances, the baby of the family, was only sixteen at the time and was too young to be allowed to go to America with her brothers.

The boys had decided to follow me out to the States and the plan was that we would sing wherever we could – gig, busk, whatever we could get. It was the only way to finance the trip.

In New York we stayed in a tiny apartment down on King Street, Greenwich Village. It belonged to a friend of the Kings, a nun called Sister Roseleen, who had gone back to Cork for the summer. And when I say tiny, I mean minuscule! All it was was one room and a bathroom. Although it was a crush, we were so glad of it and really grateful to Sister Roseleen. Shay and Michael slept on the floor and Martin and I slept in the bed. It felt just like the old days at home when we were kids, but with a bit less room!

On our first morning in New York we got up early,

grabbed our instruments and headed off to Fifth Avenue, which we knew would be a busy and fun place to start our singing adventure; we had with us Shay's guitar, Michael's banjo and mandolin, Martin's fiddle and my bodhrán and were eager to get out there and make some money busking. We soon found what we considered to be a suitable spot because the place was buzzing with activity. We quickly got a twenty-minute set together, a beginning, middle and end, so that people could listen and then move on, and we could go around with the collection boxes afterwards. We would let the crowd move off and then start the set again with a whole new crowd. This way we'd keep things moving and get more money for the time we spent on the street singing.

We were surprised at the response we got when we busked. There was a really positive energy. We would always attract a great crowd; they tended to hang around until we stopped singing and then they'd applaud and shout for more. I think the main attraction was the voices singing in harmony. Michael had a high tenor voice, Martin had a deep baritone bass voice, Shay was somewhere in the middle and I was somewhere between an alto and a soprano. It seemed very natural for each one of us to find our own harmony line when we sang together. As with many family harmony singers, the blend of our voices was always very tight. Between songs Shay would turn on the charm and tell the crowd that we were a family from Ireland and I think this appealed to the audiences even more.

Back then, in the 1970s, New York was a lot rougher than it is now and there was a lot of crime on the streets. No one bothered us, but when we busked we quickly began to spot the pickpockets as they moved through the crowd.

We soon devised a way of alerting the audiences to them, even if we were mid song. For example, instead of singing:

It was pleasant and delightful one mid summer's morn,
When the fields and the meadows they were covered with corn

we would burst into:

Be careful of your handbags and your wallets too,
Cos there is a little man who's trying to rob you.

Needless to say there were a few disgruntled thieves in and around Fifth Avenue who were hoping to make a killing from the crowd listening to our singing.

Although the busking was great fun and we did well – making around $200 a day, which was quite a bit of money back then – we had very little money to spare and were under pressure to build up a pot for day-to-day living expenses. There was also the little matter of getting enough money together for the lads' flights home.

That trip was the first time we ever really experienced inexpensive fast food, and we were grateful for it. We lived near the Italian quarter so on every corner you could go into a pizza place and buy a huge slice for a dollar or less, and it would always be the best pizza you'd ever tasted. By the end of our trip we would walk into our local place and we'd be greeted with a 'Hello, Irish!' by the big Italian man behind the counter. Needless to say, between the pizza and the great Italian ice cream I came back from the trip with an arse like the back of a bus!

There was a pub on Bleaker Street in Greenwich Village which was also a live music club called Kenny's Castaways, and the owner was Irish. This was the area where the likes of the Clancy Brothers, Bob Dylan and Joan Baez used to hang out in the 1960s. The club had an open night where anyone could go in and put their name down to sing a song or two.

At the end of each open-mic night Kenny would pick one of the acts and book them for a gig. We jumped at the chance to perform on an actual stage and on that first night we sang 'The Larks They Sang Melodious', a sea-faring song which really showed off our vocal harmonies, and 'The Broom of Cowdeknowes', a Scottish love song which again had a very powerful chorus.

We were over the moon when the Black family's name was called out as the winners. Later that night we met Kenny himself who became a good friend and looked after us well while we were in New York.

After we spent about a week busking on Fifth Avenue, someone told us about busking on the Staten Island ferry. Apparently, when people got on the ferry they all sat down, row upon row, facing the same way; it was almost like the seating in a concert hall. The journey lasted about 20–25 minutes, which was ideal for our little concert!

We decided to head down to the ferry the next day to check it out because it sounded like the perfect setting for busking.

We soon set ourselves up on the ferry and as it pulled away we burst into 'The Leaving of Liverpool':

> So fare thee well my own true love
> And when I return united we will be,
> It's not the leaving of Liverpool that grieves me
> But my darling when I think of thee

That first trip on the ferry, playing to a bunch of commuters, wasn't easy to begin with. Their initial reaction was a bit grumpy; they bowed their heads, read their newspapers or tried to close their eyes to get a few more minutes of sleep. However, by the end of the first song we knew they wanted to hear more – and by the end of the crossing they were on their feet clapping and cheering and singing along with us. We strategically placed the empty fiddle and mandolin cases at each exit and the people were very generous on their way out. We thought we were on to a winner.

As soon as the last person got off the ferry at Staten Island we grabbed our instruments and cases, which were full of coins and dollar bills, to dash on to the next ferry that was leaving. We needed to move fast to ensure we had a good spot for the journey back. Then we set up and did it all over again.

As we got off the ferry from Staten Island, ready to get on the next one over, someone asked us if we had a licence for busking. Of course, we didn't, and very suddenly the bubble burst. We were gutted. We were sitting on the pier wondering what to do next, when this lovely older man came over and asked us where we were from. He told us he was from Sligo and had left when he was a young boy and never returned. He was the captain of one of the ferries and told us whenever he was captaining we were more than welcome to perform for the passengers. This was great news to us and we became very good at giving 25-minute concerts as we travelled over and back on that ferry. This is just one example of the kindness shown to us during that trip. We met some great people who were so charmed by us they wanted to take us home, or would ask, in strong New York accents, 'Can I touch you for luck?' But really it was the Irish connection that got us through that trip. So many emigrants or first-generation Irish who knew too well what it felt like to be a foreigner in a strange land. It was those people and their Irish generosity that made all the difference to our trip.

We didn't stay in New York for the whole summer; after about a month we got a Greyhound up to Boston. From there we took a boat from Falmouth in Cape Cod across to Martha's Vineyard, a place I had always wanted to visit since I read about it when I was young. It sounded so quaint.

Knowing we had nowhere to stay on Martha's Vineyard, on the ferry over we took out our instruments and started to play, hoping that we could raise some money or that someone might offer us a bed for the night. No one was forthcoming. It was getting late in the evening when we arrived so we thought we'd check out the local bar to see if we'd have any luck there. We stuck on our charming Irish hats and played and sang for an hour or so, but there was still no one biting. I turned to Shay and said defeatedly, 'Looks like we're sleeping on the beach tonight.' Just at that moment a young woman came over to us. She seemed to be on her own and had a lot of drink onboard.

She started to tell us all about her great-grandmother

who was from Co. Kilkenny or Tipperary, or wherever, and insisted on buying us all a drink. When she found out we had nowhere to stay she invited us back to her house. Normally, we would be reluctant because she wasn't exactly sober and she said her husband and kids were asleep back at her house, which was a little weird. But the prospect of sleeping on the beach wasn't very appealing, so we decided to go for it.

When we arrived at her house she snuck us in and put us in the conservatory where there were couches and pull-out beds that we could sleep on, and we were really grateful for them.

We awoke the next morning to a man's voice roaring at the top of his lungs, 'YOU WHAT?! You brought four strangers from the bar back to our house with the kids asleep in the next room!!?'

The four of us looked at each other in horror. As quickly and as quietly as we came in, we grabbed our gear and snuck out the back door. We'd heard enough – it was time to leave.

After we fled from the house we decided to take stock and see where our next opportunity might be. It was a glorious day, so there were lots of people out and about and one of us remembered hearing that there was a fair on nearby. So we headed off in search of it and decided we'd go and busk.

We set up on a busy path and started into our set. In

the middle of singing 'Here's A Health' in four-part harmony, who should walk by but James Taylor and Carly Simon! I nearly choked mid-verse when I saw them. James smiled at us and we nodded back at him; the pair listened for a moment and dropped a few coins in the guitar case. I don't know how we made it to the end of the song but by the time we did they were gone. Little did I think many years later I would meet James Taylor at the Newport Folk Festival after he had listened to my show from the side of the stage.

It was such a memorable summer for so many reasons. It was great to hang out with my brothers and, although we had fights and laughs, we all developed as artists, that's one thing I'll say for sure.

During that summer I had completely reconciled myself to the fact that Joe and I were history. I wrote him two letters, to which I got no reply. I was gutted. He'd obviously moved on and now it looked like it was time for me to do the same.

When I arrived back in Dublin on the fifth of September I met up with my friends Marie, Caroline and Eimear in McDaids, a pub off Grafton Street. Somehow or other Joe found out I was home and arrived at the pub. He was all smiles and gave me a big hug.

For a moment I was furious – and more than a little confused. I thought to myself, who the hell does he think he is? I really felt like saying, 'Get lost!', but for some reason I kept quiet and just tried to enjoy the evening. I was home again, and that felt good. Towards the end of the night Joe kept asking me if I wanted a lift home. But I was very dismissive and kept answering, 'No thanks, I'm fine.' He obviously picked up on my coldness and eventually asked me what was wrong. I couldn't hold back and just blurted out, 'You never even answered my letters!'

He looked at me, shocked and confused, and said quickly, 'But I did! I wrote you two long letters.' Now, the one thing I knew about Joe was that he didn't lie, and I could tell he was telling the truth. I was now totally confused!

Later that night he told me how much he had missed me that summer, how much he wanted to be with me and he asked if we could give it another go.

I was reluctant to say anything initially; I didn't want to jump back into something that had caused me so much pain. I told him I would have to wait and see how I felt, although I think I already knew in my heart that he was still there and that it wouldn't be easy to walk away. Within weeks we were inseparable. It was the start of a lifelong relationship.

12

This child, he means the world to me, there is no more enchanted

It was August 1979 when Joe and I bought a run-down old redbrick house off South Circular Road on Wolseley Street, which needed a lot of work. Joe had proposed to me earlier that summer so we worked hard on that house all winter to try to get it ready before our wedding the following March, which proved more difficult than we expected.

At that point in my career I was still doing small folk gigs around Dublin which I subsidized with waitressing in a burger restaurant. General Humbert had disbanded a few months earlier so I had started doing more solo sets with Gerry O'Byrne, my guitar player, and sometimes I'd perform completely unaccompanied. Around that time, too, I was invited to do a television programme called *Christy Moore and Friends*. Christy invited some great musicians to join him in a series of gigs that was recorded and broadcast on RTÉ 1 in a primetime TV slot.

To be part of that programme was a big deal for me. While there was some awareness of me in the folk circles, this opportunity would bring me to a national audience.

I went out to the Abbey Tavern where it was to be filmed and it was great to be in the company of acts like Planxty, Ralph McTell and Paddy Keenan, and many more big names from the folk scene. I decided to sing 'Anachie Gordon', with Gerry accompanying me on guitar. It's a beautiful song that was completely unknown at the time and, as I had sung it since I was a child with Shay, I was very comfortable singing it. If you saw the recording now you'd see that I was kind of terrified, I didn't smile much and stood the whole song with my hands behind my back, but I did what I always did which was just lose myself in the lyrics and the melody of the song.

As it happened the show was broadcast the day of our wedding, the sixth of March 1980. We got married in University Church down on Stephen's Green, which was my parish church. It was a dull wet-looking day, though we were lucky as the rain stayed off.

It was still getting dark quite early so when the ceremony was over we just about got out in time to get some wedding photographs across the road beside Stephen's Green. After that Joe and I decided we'd pop into Mulligan's in Poolbeg Street, which was our local.

We went in in all our finery and had a pint of Guinness before heading off to the reception, which was in the Clarence Hotel.

I really wasn't into fancy wedding dresses. To be honest I was a bit scarlet by the whole getting married thing. I didn't want to look over the top so I wore a simple cream two-piece suit that had a knee-length skirt and fitted jacket, and a silk and lace blouse. The fanciest part of the outfit was a little cream pillbox hat with a piece of netting I sewed on myself. Joe wore a lovely brown tweed suit. My bridesmaids were Frances and Joe's sister Doll, and I told them to get any dress they wanted in a lilac colour.

Doll's real name was Catherine. Joe was seven and the youngest of three boys by the time she came along. She was a tiny baby girl and Joe's father J.P. immediately nicknamed her 'the Doll', and it stuck. Right from the start, when I first started going out with Joe, I got on well with Doll. And since Joe and I wanted the wedding to be all about family, it felt natural for my sister and Joe's sister to be my bridesmaids. Over the years, though, Doll has become much more than my sister-in-law, and today we are very close.

I really wanted my wedding to be a city wedding. I was from Dublin and I was proud of being from Dublin; I didn't want to do the whole going out to some fancy hotel on the outskirts of the city thing. I didn't like the idea of that at all, I just wanted something very played down.

There were about a hundred people at the wedding and we had a fantastic day. The food was lovely and the speeches were great. We had lots of laughs and soon the music got started, of course. However, everything came to a halt at 9.30 when the television programme was being broadcast. The whole party stopped; we found a big room that had a TV and we all squeezed in to watch me on the telly. Everyone at the wedding knew how great it was for me to get on the show and was very proud. It was great. We got back to the party and everyone sang their party piece and then some. The Black Family was, of course, all together singing, and all the people I loved were in attendance. It was just a fantastic night. So good, in fact, that nobody wanted to leave and I remember the waitress at one stage coming over and quietly saying into my ear, 'Listen, love, I don't want to spoil your day or anything, but if you don't go neither will anyone else and we have to go home!'

So we reluctantly left our own wedding and stayed in the Aisling Hotel on our wedding night up the road. We met some pals in Bewleys the next morning for breakfast, and later that night a large group from the wedding congregated at the Bunch of Grapes in Clanbrassil Street to keep the party going.

Later that year a TV-advertised album *Christy Moore*

and Friends was released on the back of the series.
'Anachie Gordon' was included and was well received.
The TV show and the album proved to be the first real
milestone in my solo career, bringing me to the
attention of a national audience.

Two days after our wedding we headed off on our honey-
moon. We had very little money at the time so we
jumped in Joe's Citroën 2CV two-seater van and set off
up to Rosses Point in Sligo. We knew we didn't have
enough money for more than a few nights, so we booked
two nights in a nice hotel. After that we drove up to
Ballycastle to spend the night there, visited Carrick-a-
Rede rope bridge and the Giant's Causeway and spent a
while looking out over to Rathlin Island. It was a really
special time – just me and Joe making plans for our
future together. On our way back down to Dublin we
decided to drop in to see my auntie Maggie in
Loughinisland, Co. Down.

Auntie Maggie, Daddy's sister, was a small woman in
her seventies, crippled with arthritis. She was definitely a
woman from another time; her grey hair was tied back in
a tight bun, and she always wore an old-fashioned cross-
over apron. She had married Johnny Rogan who was
from the area but they never had any children; when we
arrived it was like I was her daughter returning home,
and she was thrilled to see us. Johnny had died by this

time and Maggie lived in the house with his sister Maud.

That evening the best Delft was taken out for our dinner and all the food she prepared was from their own little farm. I can still remember the smell of the fresh bread she baked especially for the occasion. After the meal we tried to hit the road but Auntie Maggie insisted we stay the night. 'Ach, it's far too late for ye to be driving home now! Sure, stay the night and you can head off in the morning, we've plenty of room.'

We couldn't refuse. The bottle of sherry was dusted off and we all had a glass before bedtime. When we did eventually get into the bedroom it was even more like stepping back in time. There was an ancient brass-framed bed, a little dressing table and mirror, and a beautiful old ceramic po (a chamber pot) under the bed. There was a gorgeous old china bowl and jug for washing that must have been there for generations. When we got into the bed I noticed that the slightest movement would make the brass bed creak like mad – as if someone was jumping on it. I was mortified. Any time either of us moved the creaking would echo through the room and I would end up saying, 'Please, Joe, don't move, don't move! They'll think we're doing something!' I stayed awake most of that night, terrified I'd make a noise. Even though we were married I couldn't bear to think of what Auntie

Maggie might think we were getting up to in that bed!

Next morning it was a bit of a relief to know we were only staying the one night and I am sure, when we said our goodbyes, I must have looked wrecked from lack of sleep. But Auntie Maggie didn't say a word about it. That was the last time I saw my lovely auntie Maggie; she died later that year so I was pleased we'd taken the time to visit her.

Joe and I settled into married life and we were genuinely happy. The house we'd bought just before we got married was a three-bedroom end-of-terrace old red-brick. It didn't have a bathroom or a proper kitchen, so we roped in some friends and family to help us fix it up. My dad was retired and in his seventies but he spent all his free time plastering the house and putting all his building-trade skills to use for us. We wouldn't have been able to afford it without his help, so we owed him a lot.

In the meantime we moved into Charlemont Street. It was a particularly cold spring and it was absolutely freezing in the bedrooms at night. I remember Joe had no idea how cold it could get without central heating – which is what he was used to. Charlemont Street had nothing but an old fire-place to heat the entire house – and that was in the living room. We stayed in Charlemont Street for six weeks until our own house was habitable.

It was February 1981 when I discovered I was pregnant. Joe and I had only been married eleven months and we'd moved into Wolseley Street only the May before. We were a bit shocked, to be honest.

We had hoped to hold off on starting a family for a few years. I remember going to the doctor and getting the results, and when I was told I was pregnant I was slightly stunned. I went home and called Joe at work to tell him the news. There was a silence at the end of the phone. Eventually he said, 'Ah well . . .' I screamed at him down the phone. 'Ah well?! Is that all you can say?' I was in a bit of a panic and couldn't quite get my head around becoming a mother. I was only twenty-five, after all. But we quickly got used to the idea and began to look forward to our new arrival.

After I got married I started working in Dolphin Discs, in the bazaar on Thomas Street. I earned £40 a week selling tapes and albums. Working there really helped me to stay in touch with the music scene at the time – music from America and the UK, as well as Ireland, and the latest trad albums. I remember the John Lennon album *Double Fantasy* was out at the time and it had made a big impression on me. Later that year, when the news broke that he had been shot dead outside his apartment building in New York, I, like so many others, was very upset. I was a huge Beatles fan and I remember he had just made such a great comeback; he

Above: My mother before she was married.

Below: Daddy and Mammy with Michael, Shay and me as a baby, 1955.

Above: Auntie Frances, Granny and Mammy on O'Connell Street.

Below: Granny in the early 1960s.

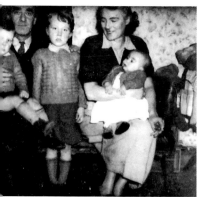

Right: On the tractor on Rathlin Island; Michael, Shay, Auntie Betty, me and Mammy, 1956.

Middle: First communion class with Sister Norbert, 1962. I'm in the second row, on the right.

Bottom: Miss Byrne's dancing class. I'm third from the left on the front row, aged about eight (and I'm still proud of the thirteen medals I won for Irish dancing).

Above left: All the family together on Martin's communion day in the hospital grounds, 1964.

Above right: Frances on her confirmation day, with me and Olive Elliott, in Charlemont Street, 1970.

Left: Me and Frances in the kitchen at the back of the shop, c.1972.

Below: My friend Robin Payne snapped this picture in Grantham Street, 1972.

Above: Having a laugh (except for me!) in our kitchen in Charlemont Sreet. *Front*: John White, Emer O'Carroll, me, Mammy and Daddy. *Back*: my brothers Michael and Martin, and Paschal Birmingham.

Below: A day's shopping in town with Olive, with our bell-bottoms and my Afro.

Above: Our wedding day, with Mam and Dad, and Joe's parents Maura and JP, Stephen's Green, 6 March 1980.

Left: Dad taking me into the church to give me away.

Below: The Black Family on stage in America, c. 1990.

Above: Holding two-week-old Róisín, 1988.

Below: Giving a talk in a north-Dublin school, c.1992. Four-year-old Róisín wouldn't let go of my hand.

Above: Conor, aged two, going to play football in the park with Joe.

Below: The first time Róisín sang on stage with me, Tokyo, c.1996.

Left: Conor on his communion day.

Above: Róisín and Danny singing at a party for my forty-first birthday in Cork.

Below: Danny raises the cup in Croke Park, 1995. (A proud granny is in the background, cheering him on.)

Above: Walking on to the stage of the Royal Albert Hall with Mammy – both of us were shocked at its size and beauty.

Below: The family at the *Circus* launch in the grounds of St Audeon's Church, summer 1995.

was giving interviews and seemed happy again, having spent five years off the scene raising his son Sean. And now it was all over for him – so tragic.

The 'black' *Planxty* album, Paul Brady and Andy Irvine and the Bothy Band albums were all popular at the time. I was also listening to Sandy Denny and Billie Holiday, both of whom I had discovered as a teenager, along with Pentangle and Steeleye Span, Dick Gaughan and Nick Jones. And from America, James Taylor, Emmylou Harris, Bonnie Raitt and Stevie Wonder.

I wasn't looking for gigs then but occasionally I'd get calls from Slattery's Bar on Capel Street, or Tailors' Hall, or the Singing Club on Thomas Street, to come and do a gig. My brothers had moved away, Michael to Limerick for college and Shay to Liverpool to find work, and I hadn't got a regular guitar player, so most of the time I'd get up and do my unaccompanied fifty-minute set.

Looking back I can't believe I sang those gigs un-accompanied. It's something I wouldn't have the nerve to do now, and when I think about it, it was a great train-ing regime for my voice. I'd get up in front of audiences of fifty to eighty people, talk about the songs and sing a set of mostly folk and traditional songs like 'Anachie Gordon', 'Bogey's Bonnie Bell', 'The Rose of Allendale' and 'Loving Hannah', which I heard from Davey Brennan and Shay. All these songs I learnt growing up, but I used to get so nervous at those gigs; for days before I couldn't eat because I felt so sick and anxious.

I was filled with self-doubt. Even though people wanted to hear me sing I felt inadequate and unworthy to be singing on a stage. I was torn because I wanted to sing but it was such an ordeal for me and I had more or less decided that performing wasn't worth the trauma I went through.

Then one day Joe said to me, 'Mary, I think you could be making a mistake; if you stop singing you might regret it later in your life.' He then quoted an old proverb: 'Don't hide your light under a bushel', and for some reason that quote hit home.

I knew he was right. I knew to be fulfilled as a person I had to face my fear and get out there and sing; somehow I just had to get over my nerves. It was around that time that I had a little talk with myself and made up my mind to try my best to conquer my anxiety. In the meantime, though, I had the birth of my first child to think about.

That summer we moved down to Courtown to work in Joe's father's pub, Fluther's. It was a really hot summer and by June my bump was huge, though I was only six months gone. Working behind the bar people would ask me when I was due, thinking it was soon, but I had a fair way to go because the baby wasn't due until September. That August I remember meeting a man in the bank in

Gorey and when he saw me he nearly passed out. He said, 'When I saw you in the pub back in June I thought you were ready to pop.' At this stage I was like a moving mountain. The pregnancy itself was fine, apart from being huge; I wasn't sick for any of it. I wish I could say as much for the birth.

I went into labour nine days overdue on the fourteenth of September. It was Joe's birthday and we were out for lunch in town. I was getting used to people staring at me, shocked at the size of my belly. Sitting down for lunch I'd see the other restaurant-goers elbowing each other and mouthing something like, '*Jazus* . . . look at the size of *that*!' That day, though, halfway through the meal, I suddenly got this strong pain and let out a loud gasp. The whole restaurant turned and gasped too. I think they thought I was going to have the baby right there! But there was no panic; we went home and I took a bath. We were both pretty calm, measuring the time between contractions and getting ready to go.

We had no car at the time so we took the bus down to Mammy's shop on Charlemont Street. At about eight-thirty that evening we got on the bus and when the conductor came to collect the fare, Joe said to him, 'We're going to the hospital, she's having a baby.' The conductor looked at me, then at my bump and turned pale. He said, 'Jesus, I hope you don't have it on the bus!'

There was great excitement when we arrived at Mammy's shop and after a while she said she'd call us a taxi. I think she was getting anxious and wanted me to get to the hospital quickly, but I said no, Joe and me were going to walk down by the canal to Holles Street Hospital. This idea really didn't go over well with her, but I thought the walk would be good for me – get things moving a bit quicker – so off we went.

At about 10 p.m. we'd got as far as Holles Street, and as I was still feeling OK I suggested we go into O'Dwyer's Pub and have a drink. Joe ordered a pint of Guinness for himself and a gin and tonic for me; someone had told me gin and tonics helped to relax you before you go into labour. We sat there for half an hour but I still felt fine so we ordered another round. It seemed like a good idea at the time!

The looks I got from people were ridiculous; they knew I was on my way into Holles Street, but I think they were frightened I might have the baby right there in the pub. After the second drink the pain started to kick in and when it became more intense we decided to head on over to the hospital. I was glad to be on my way at last, and although I knew it was going to be painful, I felt it was nothing I couldn't manage; I thought it would all be over in a couple of hours. How wrong I was!

Innocently, I was sure I could have the baby *au naturel*. Back then, thirty-two years ago, it was Holles

Street Hospital policy not to give much pain relief. It was a serious Catholic hospital and they didn't believe in epidurals or anything of the sort. Natural childbirth was the way to do it.

By one o'clock in the morning I was well and truly in the throes of labour and begging for something to numb the pain. Of course, the nuns and nurses ignored my pleas. From then on things got progressively worse. The two gin and tonics I'd had came back up pretty quickly.

By eight in the morning there was no sign of the baby, and no sign of pain relief either. I was getting really distressed, as was Joe, who held my hand, looked into my eyes and, trying to make me feel better, said, 'We needn't have any more.'

When the nurses changed their shifts it soon became clear that the new nurse on duty who was looking after me wasn't as patient or as nice as the previous one had been. She was older and very stern. After a while I thought the baby was never going to arrive, and the pain was so intense I started to think I was going to die.

Eventually, at 10.40 a.m., and weighing in at just under eleven pounds, our son Conor was born. Of course, I was very relieved – until, that is, I heard the head doctor on duty telling one of the younger doctors, 'Go ahead and suture her up, she's in a bad way.' I was so exhausted by this time his remarks didn't fully register with me, which was probably a good thing.

They gave me some local anaesthetic but as the young doctor did as he was told I could feel every needle being pulled in and out, over and over again. I told them repeatedly that it hurt like hell but they just kept saying, 'You should be numb there now.' The ordeal just went on and on, but things got even worse when the head doctor came in to check the stitches. To my horror he said, 'No, no! That's no good. They'll all have to come out.' Straight away he unstitched and re-stitched me, and once again I felt every stitch. The pain was indescribable and the whole experience was hugely unsettling for me.

Straight after this ordeal I remember being wheeled down to the newborn-baby ward. They handed me Conor, who was quite a bundle, being almost eleven pounds, and as they wheeled me back to my ward I felt so weak; I was terrified I was going to let him fall, but I didn't say anything to anyone, or complain. Back then I was afraid to say 'boo' to anyone. I think I was just so relieved by then that I had my baby. I had hoped for a boy, and here he was at last.

I was kept in hospital for six days, and on the third day I was lying in the ward looking at my baby in the cot beside me. I started looking at his face and then it dawned on me: my God, he looks as if he has Down's Syndrome. Poor Conor was so fat and had such a big round face he could hardly open his eyes. I suppose I was still recovering from the ordeal of birth and wasn't thinking straight. I was so upset and when Joe came in I had Conor in my arms and tears were rolling down my cheeks. He said, 'What's wrong?!' I was so convinced of my own diagnosis, I burst out, 'He's got Down's Syndrome!' Joe was shocked now, and I was inconsolable. He ran to talk to the sister in charge, who stormed into the room and screamed at me in her high-pitched posh accent, 'Now, Mrs O'Reilly! You have a perfectly healthy baby boy! Stop that nonsense at once!' That shut me up.

I got over the physical side of the birth quite quickly because I was young. But a few weeks after I went home I began to feel different. No energy, very distant and down. I couldn't understand why I was feeling like this. I had a beautiful healthy baby boy, a great husband and not a worry in the world. I couldn't understand it.

I used to put the TV on and stare at it for hours like a zombie. And whenever there was a news report on I felt like they were speaking directly to me. I was guilty too because I had just brought this beautiful baby into a world where terrible things were happening. I felt I couldn't protect him from any of it.

I remember there was an ad on the telly that was about a monthly magazine that taught you how to sew. 'A to Z learning without tears.' The song accompanying the ad used to go through my head twenty-four hours a day: *Busy needles, busy needles, A-Z of learning without tears.* It didn't just go through my head the way a song sometimes does when you can't get it off your mind. It would burst through my thoughts over and over again, at rapid pace like the buzzing of a bee or the way a crazy person might talk to themselves erratically in a Hollywood movie.

Around this time I found it difficult to sleep and the tiredness, combined with feeling depressed, made me feel as if I was losing my grip on reality. I tried to hide it; I tried to make myself believe that it wasn't happening. I thought I could deal with it without talking to anyone, not even Joe. I don't think Joe or the rest of the family knew what was going on with me. They might have known I was a little down, but I don't think they knew the extent of it. It never occurred to me that I might have post-natal depression and that so many other women went through the same thing following childbirth. Then, one day when Joe came home from work, I started to cry and I couldn't stop. That's when it all came out.

Looking back it was a very difficult time. It's all a bit of a haze now, so I try not to think about it too often. I was numb, and couldn't understand why I wasn't happy. It had gone on for a few months, mainly because I didn't recognize it for what it was. I also think the traumatic circumstances of Conor's birth may have exacerbated the situation. The doctor put me on medication, which did help (though, ultimately, I became dependent on it) but I think the real help came in the form of a knock on the door.

13

When Mary left her highland home and wandered forth with me

THOSE EARLY DAYS with Conor were tough for me. Though I had been on anti-depressants for a while things were still not the same. I just felt so lost, so tired all the time, one day running into the next with nothing changing. It was just a dull, monotonous routine. Since I had Conor I was doing very little in my career; I'd lacked the confidence to go back to it. And since I always found it hard to say no, I didn't even want to answer the phone in case someone might ask me to do a gig and I'd commit to something I didn't want to do.

Then it happened, quite out of the blue. Conor was about seven months old, scurrying around in his walker, which he loved, and I was cleaning around the kitchen. Joe had already left for work. There was a knock on the door and I was surprised to see Christy Moore standing on my doorstep. 'Howya, Mary?' he asked in his thick Kildare accent. 'Can I come in for a chat?'

I brought him in and made him a cup of tea. I was a bit shocked to see him; Christy was a big name in music and, although I had met him a few times, I didn't know him that well.

He played around with Conor at his feet, asked his age and how he was doing, but he cut to the chase pretty quickly: 'How would you feel about supporting me for two nights in the National Concert Hall?'

I stood there in silence, just staring at him. I was really taken aback, but also flattered; this was the biggest opportunity I'd had yet in my career. Before I had a chance to dither about whether to accept this or not, I heard myself say, 'That would be amazing, Christy . . .' And yet those dark thoughts crept into my mind: I can't do this now, I'll be terrible, I don't even have a guitar player . . . That was my out.

'But I haven't got a guitar player!' I blurted out. Straight away, Christy said, 'Sure don't worry about that, Declan Sinnott is playing with me, I'm sure he wouldn't mind playing a few songs with you.'

This was such a generous gesture from Christy, who just wanted to support me. For some reason I didn't fully understand, he believed in me and what I did. I had to do it, as frightening as it was for me in that moment; I knew I couldn't let this chance slip by.

Christy's next question was: 'What would be your

fee?' I had no idea; what the hell was my fee? I tried to make little of it. 'Ah, whatever you think is fair.' He shook his head. 'No, you have to decide what you're worth.' Of course, when he said that I had to be careful that I didn't undervalue myself, so I blurted out, 'Two hundred pounds!'

When I think of that moment now it makes me laugh out loud. What was I thinking? This was 1982; I'd worked in the record shop five days a week for £40. Now it was Christy's turn to be shocked. But he couldn't back down now – he was the one who told me to name my price!

Declan Sinnott and I started to work on songs together straight away. It wasn't the first time I had met him; he was on the scene quite a bit and had been at sessions and gigs around Dublin that I'd been to. I also knew him from the early days of Horslips, a well-known trad/rock band, where I'd seen and heard him from a distance on lead guitar. He lived in Wainsfort Road in Terenure.

I was bit apprehensive at first about going to meet him, especially as he seemed to be a bit of a rocker and I was more of a folkie. But then I was a nervous wreck about everything in those days. My confidence was rock bottom and my feeling of self-worth was at its lowest, but despite my nerves I went to the rehearsal.

Declan answered the door with a smile and a big

'Hello'. He was very friendly and made me feel at ease. And when we started going through the songs, I loved his guitar playing; we both just got into it so easily. We had a few rehearsals, but not many, and before I knew it the time had come for the first night at the concert hall.

I haven't a clue what I wore that night, but it was probably a jacket with huge shoulder pads. I loved those 1980s shoulder pads.

I remember being so nervous, but Declan was reassuring and this helped to relax me a bit before we went on stage. What struck me about the concert hall when I walked on stage was the silence. I had never sung to such a quiet audience. I was used to pubs and bars and other sessions, and there was always a buzz and a certain amount of raw energy. This was very different, very sedate in a way – and it was also the largest audience I had ever sung to.

We started into 'The Rose of Allendale':

Oh the sky was clear, the morn was fair,
No breath came over the sea,
When Mary left her highland home and wandered forth
*   with me . . .*

I closed my eyes and completely forgot where I was; I got lost in Declan's beautiful playing as he accompanied me.

My voice surprised me. Through all the depression and self-criticism, I think I had forgotten that I could actually sing, and sing well at that.

Something magical happened that night between Declan and me. At the end of that first song, we looked at each other during the huge applause that echoed around the concert hall and I think we both knew we had stumbled upon something special. I think we also knew this special thing that we had could take us forward to a new and exciting future.

It is only now that I read those first few lines of 'The Rose of Allendale' that I realize how relevant they were for that moment in my life. With Declan on stage beside me, it was as if a weight had been lifted off my shoulders; the shadows that had covered my life for those last few months had in that moment begun to recede.

Once again I felt my passion for singing and perform- ing. In fact, I think I realized then that this is what I was born to do. Although I didn't know it then, this was the start of a thirteen-year musical relationship that would take me and Declan on an amazing journey through six albums, tears, laughter and tours all over the world.

After that night Declan and I started rehearsing regularly together. We worked on a lot of songs from my repertoire and gradually added songs that Declan suggested for me. Though it didn't happen overnight, little by little my confidence returned. Singing with Declan gave me a musical purpose to focus on that I longed for. Once I had that I started to be able to appreciate family life. I could be fully present when I was with them, the anxiety subsided and I began to smile again. I had a lovely family in Joe and Conor, as well as my own personal fulfilment in the knowledge that my career was progressing.

It's hard to say whether this change was due to this new purpose I felt or the anti-depressants I'd been prescribed. When I was at my lowest I had gone to a specialist in St Patrick's Hospital. He prescribed me the anti-depressants and assured me they were non-addictive, as this was a concern of mine. I think it was a combination of the medication and singing again that brought me out of the darkness.

After about a year on the medication I decided I would wean myself off it. Soon after, to my horror, I discovered that I was suffering from withdrawal symptoms. I would get sweats, shivers and goose bumps all over my body. I couldn't understand it because I had been told these anti-depressants were non-addictive.

Despite the horrible withdrawal symptoms, because I came off the medication gradually, my symptoms were not, apparently, as bad as many others'; I later heard that patients had taken the makers of this particular anti-depressant to court for false claims relating to this matter.

*   *   *

Once I was back on track, Joe and I decided it was time for me to record my first solo album. Dolphin Records was a company that Joe's father had started in the 1960s as an offshoot of the Dolphin Discs record stores. It was home to artists like The Wolftones, Johnny McEvoy, Paddy Reilly and Sean Dumphy, and had been quite successful in the 1970s.

Joe and I felt, however, that we needed a new label for this new venture so, along with Joe's brother Paul, they started Dara Records. 'Dara', meaning 'second' in Irish, related to the fact that this label was being run by the second generation of the family. It would go on to be the biggest independent record label in Ireland, with a turnover matching the major international labels in the early 1990s.

With Dara behind us we headed into Lombard Studios on Lombard Street and spent the next couple of months in and out of the studio. Philip Begley engineered the album with a group of musicians, including Declan on guitar and keys, Donal Lunny on bouzouki and Keith Donald on sax. But it was Declan who took the reins as a musician and a producer, which was fine by me.

I was only twenty-six at the time and had very little experience of recording; I totally trusted in Declan's vision for the album. I felt lucky to have him taking on this dual role as musician and producer. He had a great way of taking an ordinary song and making it something special with his unique choice of chords and interesting arrangements. In those early days I had a lot to learn and having Declan at the helm I began a recording artist's apprenticeship of sorts that would last for the next thirteen years.

After recording the first batch of songs in late 1982 we decided to run with 'The Rose of Allendale' as the first single from the album. We were delighted with the response the song got on the radio. It wasn't just a folk song; Declan had added a country flavour on the guitar, which made it stand out as being different. It also had a strong hooky chorus that people latched on to. It was play-listed on RTÉ Radio and received a lot of air-play. This paved the way nicely for the album, which was released the following May.

It was an exciting time for me. I felt my career could really go somewhere. At the same time, though, I didn't let myself get my hopes up too much about what the future might hold. I never allowed myself to have high expectations for my career which might set me up for a fall. This was probably a defence mechanism – a kind of shield I put up that protected me from disappointment or failure in this unpredictable industry.

The self-titled album *Mary Black* charted in its first month of release and we were over the moon. It went on to win the *Sunday Independent* Arts Award For Music in 1983. I was thrilled with that award; it was the first of many that soon began to accumulate in the glass case at home. The album's success established us on the music scene and a lot of gigs around Ireland came out of it.

The following September was the first time I experienced for myself the buzz that had grown around that first album. After promoting it all summer at festivals and gigs around the country, we headed to Cork to play a headline concert at the Metropole Hotel as part of the Cork Folk Festival.

When we arrived to go on stage there were over five hundred people stuffed into the function room of the hotel, as well as people still queuing outside to get in. The management decided to open up another room where they set up more speakers so the overflow could hear the gig, even though they couldn't see us. People paid full ticket price to get into that room.

It was just me and Declan on stage, but the atmosphere was electric. We felt we could do no wrong that night. At one stage Declan and I looked at each other and shook our heads in disbelief. We had the crowd in the palms of our hands and we knew then that we had taken things to the next level.

I'll never forget that night. It was a kind of watershed moment and even now, some thirty years later, people still come up to me and tell me they were at that concert and they remember it as being a very special night.

14

And I wish I was back home in dear old Dublin

AFTER THE RELEASE of the first album, although there were more bookings for gigs coming in, money was still tight. It was late 1983, the recession was in full swing and Joe and I had a mortgage to pay.

I was approached by an advertising agency to do a photo advert for Guinness. I wasn't really into that kind of thing, selling my image and my name (especially for an alcoholic drink), but when they mentioned in passing a fee of £500 my ears pricked up. What I could do with £500 back then!

I decided to go for it and went along to the photo shoot, which was to be in a studio in town. There was a stylist there who 'fixed' my unruly hair and vetted my outfit. They were trying to recreate the look of a recording studio with the set and I was asked to sit on a stool with headphones round my neck and a glass of Guinness in my hand. I saw the ad afterwards in various magazines, like *In Dublin* and *Woman's Way*, and I was absolutely mortified. I looked like a right eejit. The caption read: *I pick up a Guinness as naturally as I pick up a tune*. While I was embarrassed by it, I was still glad of that £500.

Around that time came an offer of a different kind that was much more interesting to me. Out of the blue Alec Finn of De Dannan rang me and asked me straight out if I would like to join the band. There was no meeting, he just asked me over the phone. I was taken aback and quite flattered. De Dannan were an established band that had been touring Ireland, Europe and the States for about ten years. Alec explained that Maura O'Connell was leaving the band and they needed a new singer. My only concern was my solo work with Declan; straight away, I asked Alec if he would mind if I kept on working on my solo career when I wasn't working with them. Alec didn't have a problem with that so I gave him my answer there and then: yes, I was definitely interested.

Alec Finn (bouzouki), Frankie Gavin (fiddle), Máirtín O'Connor (accordion), Johnny 'Ringo' McDonagh (bodhrán) and Brendan O'Regan (guitar) were five amazing traditional players from Galway. I had been a fan for years and I still say that one of the best gigs I've ever seen was De Dannan at The Meeting Place in Dublin in 1979.

When Alec called he told me they were preparing to

go into the studio to record in London and they wanted me to be the singer on the album. They wanted me to sing three songs. They sent me one that they really wanted me to do called 'Song For Ireland', which was to be the title track. The two other songs were of my own choice: 'I Live Not Where I Love' and 'Paddy's Lamentation'.

A week later I got another call. This time from Maura O'Connell, who I'd never met before. She had heard I was joining the band and was calling to wish me well. She enjoyed her time with De Dannan but wanted to return to her own style of music, which was more contemporary/country influenced.

As we came to the end of the conversation she asked me, 'Can I give one piece of advice?' I said, 'Of course.' There was a short silence before she said emphatically, 'DON'T. TAKE. ANY. SHIT.'

I laughed in response, half thinking she was messing around, and we said our goodbyes. I was to realize later that it was a very valuable piece of advice.

Within a couple of weeks I was on my way to London. The first time I met the lads was in the studio. I was warmly welcomed by everyone and we got straight down to the business of the songs and their arrangements. I was in London for eight or nine days and thought I'd never get home to Conor. He was only two and I missed him something terrible.

One afternoon while the lads were doing instrument takes in the studio I took a walk around the shops in the area. At one point I saw a mother with a little boy in a buggy. I couldn't believe how much he looked like Conor; he looked about the same age with the same colour hair, he was even wearing a little green and blue outfit from Mothercare that I had bought for Conor. I must have been in some sort of hormonal motherly state because I kept trying to get glimpses of him. I knew it wasn't actually Conor, but it was like I was in a trance and just wanted to look at this child. I realized after about fifteen minutes of following this woman around the shop that I was acting like a stalker and the woman was beginning to notice. I walked away feeling even worse than before. It was the first time I'd been separated from my child but I think I knew even then that this feeling of yearning was something I'd have to learn to live with if I wanted a singing career. And I was right. That longing for my children was something I would carry with me throughout my career and it would never get any easier.

The following March I headed off to America with the band. It was a three-week tour from coast to coast. I realized quickly that Frankie and I didn't see eye to eye. He would sometimes talk to me as if he was my boss and as far as I was concerned, when it came to the songs I sang, I was my own boss. It wasn't that we had rows or anything, there was just a feeling of tension between us about certain issues. One night, at the end of the first week of the tour, we had our set list made out as usual and had agreed that there would be one tune and one song for the encore. I stood side of stage during the tune waiting to be called out for the song. But as the huge applause roared from the audience Frankie burst into another set of tunes. They then took their bows and came off stage. I couldn't believe it and I was furious. After being a part of the whole show to be excluded at the end was belittling.

I don't lose my temper very often but when I do people know about it. Maura's words echoed through my mind. What had just happened wasn't what made me so angry; it was a culmination of different occurrences really, but this was the straw that broke the camel's back. I marched into Frankie's dressing room after the show, looked him straight in the eye and said, 'How dare you! I am not going to be walked on, and for two pins I'll be on the next plane home.'

Frankie was gobsmacked, to say the least. He had never seen this side of me and I don't think he expected it. He immediately apologized and said he wasn't think-ing. We sat down after that and talked about our differences and generally cleared the air. From that moment on we got on like a house on fire and never had another row. This was another good lesson and one that has remained with me: in this industry it's important to stand up for yourself to get the respect you deserve.

Singing in De Dannan taught me a lot about performance. Because the band were so good at what they did I had to give every song I sang my absolute best in order to get the same response from the audience (I've always had a competitive streak). I learnt that it's not enough to be a good singer; you have to put your heart and soul into every performance and take nothing for granted.

It was after my first tour with De Dannan that Declan began to occasionally come up with ideas to record that, in my view, did not make financial sense. We had tried one or two of these ideas that, as far as I was concerned, didn't seem to work out and so for a period we didn't see eye to eye on a few projects. So, for a short time we went our separate ways.

It was during this time that Joe had the idea to pull together a compilation of songs I had recorded, which we would call *Collected*. We recorded four new tracks for the album and P.J. Curtis produced them. My good friend and great guitar player Pat Armstrong played guitar instead of Declan. The songs we collected were from the more folk-traditional side of my repertoire, three from the De Dannan album, and three from the album *General Humbert II*. It was released in 1984 and it did OK, considering there was no single release or live gigs to promote the album. We had no great expectations about it, we just wanted to get it out there.

Soon after that Declan and I sorted out our differences and got back on track to recording the next studio album. He was only absent for a couple of months but I was glad to have him back as I felt a little lost without him.

After about a year and half of touring *Song For Ireland* with De Dannan, my second son Danny was born in March 1985. In contrast to Conor's birth it was relatively easy as I had an epidural and he was only nine pounds (my smallest baby). Unlike Conor, he had more of my colouring, black hair and huge blue eyes. I was delighted I had another boy because I was so besotted with Conor; he was such a good baby, and if Danny was anything like him I'd be doing well.

The day we brought Danny home was the day that Conor stopped being so good! I walked into the house and introduced him to his baby brother. He was a dote at first; three-year-old Conor kissed Danny on the forehead and said, 'He's lovely.'

This lasted for about five minutes. After feeding Danny and changing his nappy I started walking around the house with him in my arms. Out of the blue, Conor said, 'OK, Mammy, it's time to put the baby down now.' I explained that I couldn't put him down because I was trying to wind him and with that he burst into tears.

Through sobbing breaths he shouted, 'I hate that baby! I wanna throw that baby out the window!'

Danny got frightened by Conor's sudden outburst and started crying too. Once the two kids started, I for some reason couldn't stop myself from crying too. Joe ran in when he heard all the commotion and didn't know who to go to first!

Because I had committed to a three-week tour with De Dannan that May, it meant I had to leave Danny when he was only eight weeks old. This was heartbreaking for me but I knew I was leaving him in capable hands. My mother had agreed to look after the boys during the day while Joe was at work.

Just before we left, Dolores Keane, who was a founding member of the band, rejoined us. Everyone was delighted to have us both in the line-up and Dolores and I hit it off immediately. She had a great sense of humour and would have me in stitches laughing every day on tour. This helped during the day but at night time it was more difficult – that's when I felt really miserable. I would lie awake at night just thinking about my kids and missing them so much. Dolores and I always shared a room and when I met her recently she reminded me of a story from that tour.

She noticed that I was very quiet one day. The lads

noticed, too, and asked her what was wrong with me. She told them that I was probably just missing the kids and not to bother me. She was right. When we got back to the hotel that night I didn't really want to talk, I just wanted to get into bed and turn out the light. I lay there for a while until I suddenly sat up in the bed and called out her name.

She turned on the light and asked, 'What is it, loveen?'

I turned to her with tears streaming down my face and sobbed, 'I can't see Danny's face!' I lay in bed that night thinking of my family. I could visualize Conor's face, Joe's face, my mother's face, even Eoghan and Aoife, Frances's kids . . . but for some reason I couldn't bring Danny's image to mind no matter how hard I tried. This made me hysterical. What sort of mother was I that I couldn't picture my own son's face? Dolores tried to console me as best she could and eventually I calmed down and went back to sleep. She had no kids at the time, but she never forgot how heartbroken I was and I'll never forget how grateful I was to have her on that tour with me.

Alongside my work with De Dannan, which was sporadic, I knuckled down to record my second solo album, *Without The Fanfare*. Declan and I had decided to go a different route for this record, introducing drums, electric bass and generally a more electric sound. After the first album we weren't really sure what direction we wanted 'Mary Black' to go in. I didn't want to be restricted to singing only folk and traditional music; we both had a broad interest in different genres and wanted to experiment a little.

I remember talking to Declan about it at the time and he suggested, 'Let's just shake the tree and see what falls.' I suppose we were the trees and 'what falls' were the various musical apples! This shaking of the tree included a change in style of repertoire too. It was the first time I actively used contemporary Irish songwriters. It included songs from Jimmy MacCarthy, Noel Brazil, Mick Hanley and Declan himself and there wasn't a traditional song in sight.

Without The Fanfare was released in 1985. We took the musicians who had played on the album on a tour around Ireland. Declan, myself, Eoin O'Neil (electric bass), Nollaig Bridgeman (drums), Carl Geraghty (sax) and Philip Begley. Philip had never performed live but played some keys on the album and had also engineered it, so we decided to take him with us.

We opened the tour with a show in the Olympia Theatre, Dublin, did two weeks around Ireland and then came back to Dublin to finish the tour with another night at the Olympia. It was great fun, and a musical departure from anything we had done before. Strangely, the one song that stands out in my mind on that tour was a cover we did of 'The Things We Said Today' by The Beatles. When we came back on stage for the encore all of us stood around one mic with just Declan on the guitar. We really had to talk Carl into doing it. He told us he was 'a sax player not a singer' but I sweet-talked him around. It wouldn't have had the same effect if we didn't all do it. Swaying and clicking our fingers to the music, we sang the whole song in four-part harmony. In that moment I realized how much easier it is on stage when you are surrounded by other musicians. It made being away from home easier too, as you had your 'tour family' around you.

After that tour I was rarely without a band when I performed and I enjoyed the feeling of support and collaboration.

Without The Fanfare was received well but not quite as well as we had hoped. Both Declan and I felt that maybe we had gone too far in that electric direction. It just didn't feel quite right to us.

However, I think we needed to make that journey in order to find the right path to take going forward. We needed to push our musical boundaries to discover where we felt most comfortable. That was somewhere between our first release, *Mary Black*, which was fairly traditional, and *Without The Fanfare*, and we would strive to find it with our next album.

* * *

Declan and I were becoming more and more in demand for gigs following the release of the second album but I began to feel there was a conflict between my work with De Dannan and my solo career. Sometimes when I was with De Dannan I would be asked by the audience to sing songs from the Mary Black catalogue and vice versa. This began to bother me. They were two very different styles, but at the same time I couldn't separate them.

On top of all this, life was getting really hectic, with two small children at home to raise and two bands to tour and record with. Something had to go and in a way the decision was easy. I wasn't about to give up either more time with my kids or my solo career so De Dannan was the only option.

With a heavy heart I told the band that I was leaving. It was a hard thing to do as I felt I had made lifelong friends in Dolores and the lads. I loved working with De Dannan; it was an invaluable experience that would stand me in good stead for the rest of my life, but I knew it was the right time to leave, and I was ready to give my all to my solo career.

I had been a fan of Sandy Denny's since I was about eighteen. There was something about her voice and the way she sang that drew me in. As I delved deeper into her repertoire I also found out that she was a great writer.

She sang with a well-known English folk/rock band

from the 1960s and 1970s called Fairport Convention. One of my favourite albums of theirs was *Liege & Leif*, which I listened to over and over as a teenager. 'Crazy Man Michael' was one of the songs on that album, which I subsequently recorded on the first General Humbert album back in 1975. Sandy had a very powerful influence on me and inspired me. So much so that when I would get really nervous on stage I would close my eyes and think of her. Tragically she died in an accident in 1978. She was just thirty-one years old and, sadly, I never got to meet her or hear her sing live. Somehow, it felt right that 'By The Time It Gets Dark', written by her, became the title track of my next album.

In preparation for *By The Time It Gets Dark*, Declan and I decided to do some demos in Tadhg Kellegher's studio in Ballyvourney, Co. Cork.

Declan had got to know some musicians from Cork, where he was living at the time, and he enlisted Pat Crowley, a piano and accordion player from Kinsale, to come and join us.

There was always an aura of enthusiasm and energy when working with Pat. The first time I met him was when I walked into Tadhg's studio and he greeted me with a huge smile; he seemed eager to get started on recording. There was a seriously Spanish look about him, with his shoulder-length curly black hair, thick moustache and sallow skin. We laughed together about our shared dark looks and talked of the Spanish Armada landing on the coasts of Ireland in the 1600s and how they'd left their mark on the local women.

Once we started working together I very quickly realized that Pat was an amazing musician. Apart from his obvious musical ability he had a sensitivity for the music that mirrored my own. He instinctively felt the emotion of the songs and his playing really moved me. He was to become a lifelong friend and a loyal and permanent presence on my left-hand side on stage throughout my career.

Everything was going well with the recording sessions but in one of the demos we thought it might be nice to use a double bass. We asked Tadhg if he knew a double bass player in the area, and in his strong Cork accent he turned towards the window, pointed and said, 'Well, the carpenter that's working outside there plays double bass.'

'Great,' I said. 'Get him to bring it in tomorrow.'

Tadhg McCarthy (the carpenter) brought in his bass the next morning and we loved the sound of it. Declan and I both agreed that this was the sound that we wanted on this album.

After demoing we came to Dublin and started recording the album in Lansdowne Studios. Alongside Declan and Pat we enlisted Garvan Gallagher from Glenageary to play double bass, Mick Daly on mandolin, and Carl

Geraghty guested on the song 'Katie' on sax. Written by Jimmy MacCarthy, this was the first single from the *By The Time It Gets Dark* album. It was a huge success for me and was in the Top 10 singles chart that Christmas. Subsequently 'Once In A Very Blue Moon' was released as a single and became a radio hit, and this helped keep the album high in the charts. This album was a stepping-stone on our musical journey and I've always been very proud of it.

Despite this success, Declan and I knew there were more layers to be unravelled and developed. In a sense, this felt like just the beginning, because although the album did really well and I was very happy with what we produced, there was a part of me that felt we could take the music further. I wasn't sure where exactly that was, but I was soon to find out.

15

Oh weren't them the happy days

I AM SITTING in the busy front bar of Ryan's Pub on Queen Street, Dublin, surrounded by my family and friends. It is a warm Friday night in June 1986 and sitting either side of me are my four siblings. Michael has just got back from a year of studying in California and Shay is home for a few weeks' holiday from Liverpool. It is a rare occasion that the five of us sit around a table like this any more. But when we do get the chance it is something we all cherish. I sit silently in that corner as Michael breaks into the first verse of 'The Broom of Cowdeknowes',

> *How blithe each morn' was I to see,*
> *My lass come o'er the hill,*
> *She skipped the burn and ran to me,*
> *I met her with good will . . .*

As he strums lightly on the guitar, his tenor voice

carries over all the noises of the pub until everyone hears it and goes silent. Gradually his friend Jerry Laws joins in gently on the banjo; he knows this song well, he's heard Michael sing it since their days in Guinness's together. Michael comes to the first line of the chorus and is joined by the voices of Shay, Martin, Frances and myself. We do not need to be asked to sing, nor do we need to be told what or when to sing. We all know the words and what harmonies to take, though we have never really sat down together and practised.

Singing at sessions like this has always been our 'practice', with Michael singing the main melody and the four of us singing in harmony with him; Frances sings an octave above him, Shay takes the high harmony, Martin takes the lowest harmony available, while I slot in my harmony somewhere between Shay and Martin. Our voices merge seamlessly.

As I look across at the faces in the bar as I sing, I catch sight of my parents. My mother has just turned seventy and my father is looking as frail as I've seen him at the ripe age of seventy-six. But watching them sitting there together, singing along eagerly with their five children, they could not have looked happier or more proud. Seeing their faces, and the faces of most of my close family and friends as they listen intently, also made me listen closely to our voices. In a way, singing with my family was always something I took for granted. While I always loved doing it, it was something that just came naturally to us; at times I don't think we appreciated what a gift this was that we had.

It was later that night that Joe sat down next to the five of us. While Joe loved music he tended to stand on the outskirts of a session for fear he might be asked to sing. At that point, though, there was a break in the songs and he came over to have a chat.

One subject had been mentioned in passing before, but that night Joe brought it up again. 'Listen, lads, is it not time the five of you made an album?'

We all looked at each other then and nodded in agreement with him. The time felt right.

Martin said with a smile on his face, 'Sure we should do it for posterity. Our grandchildren will appreciate it,' and we all agreed.

Once we made the decision to do it we didn't hang around; we started recording the album that summer in Nicky Ryan's studio in Artane. Nicky had worked as an engineer for the traditional band Clannad for many years and had a lot of experience in recording. We recorded it over a period of two weeks. We literally picked all the songs we sung at sessions, the songs that came naturally to us, so there was no drama about the arrangements as we had been singing many of these songs together since we were kids.

As in any family, though, there were rows and

disagreements – the type of rows you only have with your brothers and sisters. The politeness and decorum you might have with others goes out the window when you're working alongside people who know the bones of you. You never worry about speaking out of turn, and at the same time you don't worry about looking silly or making a fool of yourself. I think there were times Nicky thought the rows we were having were getting pretty serious, and he would be dumbfounded when, ten minutes later, we were cracking up laughing and joking with each other.

Michael and Shay had to leave Ireland straight after recording, so I did a lot of mixing afterwards with Nicky. I remember one particular night when we were mixing 'Will Ye Gang'. Nicky kept saying to me, 'I can hear a sixth voice! What is that? Can you hear it?' I agreed – there seemed to be an extra harmony on top of the five voices. For a little while we were a bit freaked out, thinking it might be some sort of eerie ghost voice. Then we realized that it wasn't another voice but a harmonic; this happens when a number of notes come together in harmony and create another tone of sorts. It was the first time I had come across it.

The Black Family album was released later that year and subsequently we got a slot on the *Late Late Show*. We were thrilled when we got this opportunity. It was the week before Christmas, so there couldn't have been a better time for us to do it. Back then there was hardly a soul in Ireland who would miss the *Late Late* on Friday night. It was the most watched show in the country.

I remember clearly how the five of us stood in a semi-circle on the stage and belted out, unaccompanied, 'Colcannon', a song we learnt from our Auntie Frances. It's a traditional song that reminisces about the food that mothers used to make. I stood there with the others each side of me and started in to the first verse; their voices joined mine in harmony as I reached the rousing chorus:

Oh you did! So you did!
So did he and so did I,
And the more I think about it
Sure the nearer I'm to cry,
Oh weren't them the happy days,
When troubles we knew not,
And our mothers made colcannon in a little skillet pot.

Gay Byrne, the host, came over for a quick chat after the song. He introduced us all by name to the audience and said, 'And I hear your mother and father are here tonight, too?' Just then the cameras zoomed in on them and they waved at us enthusiastically. They were as proud as Punch. He called to them in the crowd saying, 'Well, Mr and Mrs Black, you must be very proud!'

It's funny how that moment sticks out in my mind

so much. The fact that it was a significant event that I got to share with my whole family made it all the more special.

People really responded to that performance. I suppose it wasn't something the general public were used to seeing on mainstream television: a family getting up and singing a traditional song in harmony completely unaccompanied. There was no grandeur to our performance either, we just got up and sang our hearts out with our hands placed firmly behind our backs or in our pockets, as if we were standing in the corner of a pub.

We didn't go on tour immediately with the album as it was difficult with the lads living abroad, but we did have two gigs in the Baggot Inn the following weekend. This was a fairly dingy lounge bar at that time, but it had become a famous venue for live music over the years.

We weren't really expecting much as this was our first album together, but when we arrived for the show there was a queue out the door and around the block to get into the gig. Both nights were sold out.

Because of the success of those two gigs we started to think about the possibility of touring around Ireland the following summer. Pat Egan, my promoter at the time, got on board and booked us ten or twelve dates, starting with a night in the National Concert Hall in Dublin. We were all a bit nervous; this would be the biggest venue we'd ever appeared at.

After the sound check Frances decided she would go home to shower and change as she lived not too far away. We were to be on stage at eight o'clock but by half seven there was still no sign of Frances.

After a few phone calls to Shay's wife Anne who had gone with her, we were told that she felt she couldn't do the gig. Frances had split up with her husband a couple of months earlier. She was living in a tiny bedsit at the time and was finding the separation very hard; Christmas had been difficult for her both financially and emotionally with two small babies. She'd had an argument with her ex that day, and was really struggling at the time. She says herself she feels she was on the verge of a breakdown.

I think in truth the thoughts of a gig in the National Concert Hall was just extremely nerve-racking for her; she was only twenty-five, the youngest of the family, and hadn't by then clocked up as much experience in performing as the rest of us. At that time I wasn't really aware of what was going on; I had no patience for it and was getting madder by the minute because this was an important night for us. We paced the room hoping that she would do the gig and at ten to eight we got the call that said she was on her way. We breathed a sigh of relief.

Before she arrived, Shay said to me, 'Now, Mary, calm down. Don't say a word to her when she comes in or she'll just get upset again.'

Frances walked in the door with red eyes just five minutes before we were due to go on.

The room was silent for a second and before I could stop myself I shouted, 'What the hell are you playing at?!'

With that she burst into tears and bolted for the toilet, locking the door behind her. Why couldn't I keep my big mouth shut? I ran after her and said through the bathroom door, 'I'm really sorry, Fran, I just couldn't help myself, come on, come out.' The answer I got was indecipherable through her tears and sniffles.

The four of us and Anne tried in turn to persuade her to come out, but to no avail. It was eight o'clock and the stage manager was calling us to the stage.

We tried to put it off for as long as we could but by five past eight the audience had started a slow handclap and we couldn't wait any longer. Shay, Michael, Martin and myself reluctantly walked on stage without our sister and started into 'Donkey Riding'.

After our first two songs Frances slipped on to the stage without saying a word and just blended in as if she'd been there all along. We went down a storm and Frances sang as well as I'd ever heard her. All was forgotten as we took our bows to rapturous applause.

I didn't realize it then, but Frances was going through rough times. I'm sad that I didn't know it at that point; I would have been more supportive if I'd known what the real problem was, rather than having my annoyed big sister hat on. I'm happy to say that she pulled herself through that hard time and we are able to laugh about that night together now; a typical day in the life of the Black family.

16

'No Frontiers'

IN JANUARY 1988 Joe and I discovered to our surprise that I was pregnant for the third time. It was a bit of a shock, as we weren't planning on having another baby at that time. There was a major four-week tour of the US and Canada coming up in April and by then I would be nearly five months pregnant.

For a while we seriously considered cancelling the tour. Though I was only thirty-two, I thought I was getting old! Touring was tough enough without being pregnant and this tour was shaping up to be pretty gruelling. However, I decided to go ahead with it. I never liked letting people down and as I'd committed to it I felt I should do it.

Back then, touring North America involved getting up very early, flying to the next city, sound-checking, eating and gigging. There was very little time for rest but I took it where I could. Very often it would be in an airport where I'd lie down on the floor with a bag under my head until someone told me the flight was boarding. I didn't care how I looked or who saw me, sometimes I just had to get my head down.

When the tour began I was four and half months pregnant and was hoping that my bump wasn't too obvious when I was on stage. I was a private person and wanted to keep my pregnancy that way. I would hide it by wearing loose clothes, but within a week of touring I sprouted.

I thought I would never get to the end of that tour; it seemed to go on for ever and I found it physically exhausting. The last concert was in Toronto and I think I already looked about six months pregnant at that stage. I just needed to be home and when I eventually got there I stayed put. I had most of the summer off to spend with Joe and the boys and to prepare for the new arrival.

During that summer, Declan and I had plenty of time to think about the next album. We were happy with the direction we took for *By The Time It Gets Dark*, but we were always eager to move forward, try new things and generally develop our music.

Jimmy MacCarthy had been on to Declan saying he had some new songs, so we invited him over to my house in Harold's Cross (where I'd moved to from Wolseley Street) to hear them.

He arrived on a warm day that summer and the three

of us had a cup of tea together in my kitchen. When he took out his guitar and began to sing I was rooted to the spot.

> *If life is a river and your heart is a boat,*
> *And just like a water baby, baby, born to float,*
> *And if life is a wild wind that blows way on high,*
> *And your heart is Amelia; dying to fly.*

As Jimmy came to the end of the song the three of us sat together in silence. I was very moved by what I'd just heard. I felt so in awe of Jimmy having the gift to write such a beautiful song. I loved it straight away. It was everything that I looked for in a song; it had beautiful lyrics and an interesting melody that weaved its way through each verse before it arrived at a simple two-line hook:

> *Heaven knows No Frontiers*
> *And I've seen heaven in your eyes.*

As an artist who doesn't write much of my own material it's hugely important for me to feel the emotion behind the songs I sing so that I can do them justice. If someone played me a truly brilliant song but for some reason it stirred no grand feelings in me, I would regretfully decline to sing it. If I hear a song for the first time and it moves me I know I can convey that emotion to an audience. It's not necessarily the difference between a good song or a bad song, it's how it makes me feel that leads me to the songs I sing. I need that kind of connection.

I knew from the moment Jimmy put the guitar down that this song was perfect for me. I couldn't wait to get my hands on it! I also knew from the look on Declan's face that he felt the same. Little did we know then that this song would play a huge part in the next album, which would open doors and lead us to new horizons around the world.

That summer Mick Hanly had sent us a great song too. 'Past The Point of Rescue' was totally different from 'No Frontiers', more up tempo and energetic, and we knew it would be a great single for radio.

We recorded it in August in Ropewalk Studios in Ringsend. There was such a buzz in the studio during that session. With Declan on guitar, Pat on accordion, Garvan Gallagher on bass, Nollaig on drums, Mick Daly on mandolin and Carl on sax, we felt we had discovered a new sound and this song was a great start to the next album.

'Past The Point of Rescue' was released that autumn and got a great deal of radio play and quickly became a hit in Ireland. Meanwhile I had to get down to the business of having this massive baby that was ever growing inside me. My bump was so big I was convinced it would be another boy and was too afraid to wish for a girl in case I was disappointed. Don't get me wrong; I love my boys to bits, but a girl would have been the icing on the cake for me and Joe.

When I was a week overdue I was brought in to be induced at the Rotunda Hospital on the twenty-eighth of September, and when the baby was born and Dr McKenna looked at me and said, 'You have a little girl!', Joe and I were over the moon. Róisín Patricia (after my mother) was 10lb 15½oz. Though she was an ounce heavier than Conor, she wasn't chubby like he was. She was extremely long for a baby and had these long limbs and fingers, a bit like spider's legs. She was the most beautiful baby I had ever seen. After two gorgeous boys it felt so perfect to have a girl.

Four weeks later I was on the *Late Late Show* singing 'Past The Point of Rescue'. Gay Byrne congratulated me on my 'eleven-pound baby girl' and the audience gasped and applauded.

Work started on the new album at Windmill Lane Studios in Ringsend in April 1989. For an album that brought so much success, it was probably the hardest one I ever recorded. But being in the studio suited me, as I was able to get home every night to Róisín and the boys. Dan Fitzgerald engineered the album. He

Above: Declan Sinnott and me on stage, c. 1991 (Black and Decky).

Below: The band and crew in Japan for our first Japanese tour; Yoko and Fujimoto in front, centre.

Above left: Dave Early doing his take of Battlin' Jack Champion.

Above right: Dave in character again in Australia with Máire Ní Chathaisigh, Carl, Pat, Donal Lunny, and the back of Maura O'Connell's head.

Ballyvourney, *c. 1994. Left to right*: Carl Geraghty, Dave Early, Garvan Gallagher, Me, Pat Crowley, Frank Gallagher, Declan Sinnott.

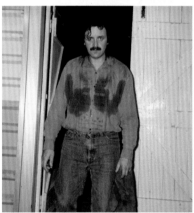

Above left: Trevor Plunkett doing his Michael Flatley impersonation on a sleeper bus, c.1995.

Above right: Me with Barbara Kenny in Cincinatti.

Left: Pat coming off stage after a steaming gig at the Dome in Tralee – still with me after twenty-eight years!

Below: Meeting Bill Clinton for the first time, after singing 'Song for Ireland' outside the Bank of Ireland on Dame Street, Dublin.

Left: Joe and Hazel (Reynolds) O'Connor from the office at the *Holy Ground* album launch doing their 'What a company!' chant, 1993.

Below left: Maeve Kearney and Pat Armstrong, early 2000s.

Below right: Celebrating with Conor after a big championship win for Templeogue Synge Street.

Bottom: With Shane Howard in Australia in 1992.

Above left: Me and my big brother Shay backstage after a gig in England, c.1996.

Above right: Outside the sleeper bus on one of the many American tours, early 2000s. *Back*: Pat, Billy, Pat Armstrong, James Blennerhassett, Martin Ditcham, Bill, Liam McCarthy (lights), driver, Damian McCollum. *Front*: fan and Alec McGinley.

Right: In Ballyvourney studio, west Cork. Steve Cooney, Dave Early, Billy Robinson, me and Frank Gallagher. Steve dropped in on the recording session with a bucket of fresh prawns.

Below: On stage with Bill Shanley . . . still playin' together after nineteen years.

Above left: With Eleanor McEvoy on the road, 1991.

Above right: Singing at the Newport Folk Festival with Joan Baez, c.1997.

Above: 'Bringing it All Back Home', TV filming in Nashville with EmmyLou Harris and Dolores Keane, 1991.

Left: With Van Morrison and Donal Lunny after a recording for the Sult television series, c.1997.

Left: Róisín on stage with her band, 2012.

Above: Singing with Frances onstage – not sure when or where.

Below: One of the many Olympia gigs, *c.* 2006; Danny did support and joined me for the finale.

Left: A break from recording the album *Full Tide* in Kerry. **Back**: Billy Robinson, James Blennerhassett, Bill Shanley. **Front**: Pat Crowley, me and Martin Ditcham.

Middle: Men in suits . . . with the band in New York in 2010. **Left to right**: Nick Scott, Neil Drinkwater (standing in for Pat Crowley), Richie Buckley, Bill Shanley, Martin Ditcham.

Bottom left: Two handfuls of love – granddaughters Fía and Bonnie.

Bottom right: Me and Joe having a laugh in the midst of all the craziness.

had been doing our live sound since the mid-1980s.

While the songs and musicianship flowed better than ever, there was an atmosphere of discontent among Declan, Dan and the band. Declan as producer had his own vision for the album but the band felt that he didn't give them enough space or opportunity to express themselves as artists; he was more or less telling them what to play.

I actually don't think Declan was aware how bad things were until it all came to a head. The line between the producer and engineer was blurred and this resulted in mounting tensions too between Declan and Dan. I also think Declan thought Dan was trying to cross that line, taking on a producer's role, and he felt that things needed to be more defined.

Words were had between them and Dan stood up and walked out halfway through recording. He eventually came back but in the meantime, tensions were building again between Declan and the other band members. When each member of the band did a take on their respective instruments, Declan would often say, 'No, that's not it, that's not what I'm looking for.' And yet he would not be able to tell them exactly what it was he wanted. This was very frustrating and, quite understandably, it peeved off the band.

In fairness I knew where Declan was coming from, too. He was mainly concerned about producing a great album, no matter what. He was so focused on the music I don't think he knew how hard he was being on the lads. Pat turned around at one stage and threw up his hands, said he was finished and walked out of the studio. I ran after him and pleaded with him. 'Please stay, Pat, just stay and finish out the album.' I stood behind Declan as he was my musical partner and producer but I really didn't want to lose Pat because he was such a great player. To be honest all I wanted was harmony so we could get on with it and make a good album. I think Pat felt bad for me and didn't want to let me down, so he eventually came back.

On returning to the studio after that bust-up the air had cleared and the atmosphere got better.

The feeling on the last day in the studio was fantastic. I was thrilled that we'd come through all the ups and downs and still managed to come out the other side having achieved what we set out to do. But just when I thought we were out of the woods another setback came our way.

During recording Declan and I decided we'd leave out a section of the song 'No Frontiers' because we felt it was a little long; we thought we'd go straight into the last chorus and leave four lines out. To us, it just seemed to flow better that way. Just before the album was released to the public, Declan played the recording of 'No Frontiers' to Jimmy MacCarthy. Jimmy, of course, then realized that lines had been left out and he was very upset by it. It wasn't the way he had written the song. Soon after that we were notified by Jimmy's solicitor that we couldn't release the album with 'No Frontiers' on it recorded the way it was. In law, there is that provision that the first recording of a song must meet with the approval of the writer. If you cover a song subsequent to the first recording, it can be changed, but the first recording has to have the go-ahead of the writer.

Initially we were annoyed with Jimmy for doing this to us. The album was recorded and the artwork was complete; we had a release date and 'No Frontiers' was to be the title track. Now, because of Jimmy's objection, we had to go back into the studio, which involved getting all the musicians and engineers back together, to re-record the song, which then had to be mixed and mastered once again. Back then it was very difficult to change and edit finished songs. This was before digital recording, when everything was done on analogue tape. If you wanted to edit the tape you had to get a blade and literally cut it and then add in more tape. It was an arduous and risky process.

Luckily we had the expertise of Philip Begley to cut up the tape for us. He spliced four bars from the backing track, inserted them into the original recording and I sang the four lines over it:

And heaven has its way
When all will harmonize,
And know what's in our hearts,
The dream will realize . . .

After singing those lines in the studio I realized Jimmy was right. They were an integral part of the song and I don't know what we were thinking leaving them out. Cutting the tape in this way meant that we didn't have to re-record the whole song. Jimmy's solicitors were sceptical about the way we were trying to add the lines but when they heard the amended recording they couldn't hear the edit so they gave us the go-ahead with the album.

No Frontiers was released in August 1989 and was in the Top 30 for fifty-six weeks and generated triple-platinum sales. It was this album that brought my career to a new level. The sound quality of *No Frontiers* was considered so good that *What Hi-Fi?* magazine used it as an audiophile reference when testing high-end speaker set-ups, which was a great compliment to my voice and the music. More than that, though, it was the album that launched me on an international scale.

One evening not long after we launched the album Joe was leaving the office in Ship Street when the phone rang. On the other end of the line was a voice he had never heard before. In a midwestern drawl a man said, 'Hi there, could I speak to Joseph O'Reilly please?' It was Bill Straw calling from Curb Records, a record label in LA; Bill's own label, Gifthorse, was part of the Curb Records Group based in Nashville.

Bill told Joe he'd heard 'No Frontiers' on the radio the day before and straight away he said he loved my voice; it had such an impact on him that when he first heard it he rang PBS Radio to find out who the singer was and then tracked down the album. He told Joe there and then he wanted to sign me for his label and that he was coming to Dublin as soon as he could to talk to him about it.

New Frontiers
Denise Sofranko, Dirty Linen #32 Feb/Mar 1991
1 March 1991

When Gifthorse Records' founder Bill Straw first heard Mary Black's voice on a Los Angeles public radio station, he knew he was hearing something special. 'I spun around and turned the radio up. When I heard her I knew I had to get that album. We had it by that night and I listened to it and immediately got right on the phone to Ireland.'

Bill flew over to Dublin and by the end of the week the deal was done; we signed the contract in Crowley

Miller Solicitors in Dublin and afterwards Joe, Bill and I went next door to O'Dwyer's Pub on Mount Street to celebrate. When we ordered our drinks there was a guy setting up keyboards in the corner and doing a little sound check. It was a stroke of serendipity when he launched into 'No Frontiers' as his first song. The three of us fell about the place laughing and Bill said, 'Hey, it's a standard already!'

It was an exciting time for me – a time of new opportunities and new beginnings. Up until then we had no record deals outside of Ireland and our music was exported through Irish companies to the few diehard fans abroad. This was our big chance to break into the American market and things began to move really fast.

17

Remember when we walked on hills of heather

A VIOLENT WIND sweeps the hair around my face while my fingers cling to the wooden bench I'm sitting on as I try to keep my balance. It is the first time I have made the journey to Rathlin Island and I wished that I wasn't going there. It is the thirtieth of January 1990 and the sea between Rathlin and Ballycastle is as rough as I've ever seen it. The ominous grey clouds overhead look as if they're ready to burst at any moment. In a way, they mirror the faces around me. Sitting beside me are my brothers and sister, my sons and Joe, my niece and nephew and my mother. In front of me lies my father's coffin.

Daddy was diagnosed with lung cancer in early 1989. He had smoked Player's untipped cigarettes for most of his life and at the age of seventy-nine it caught up with him. He deteriorated quite quickly and by

Christmas that year his mind was beginning to go. Shay and Michael came home to see him as they knew he hadn't long left.

One day in December that year I called in to see him. He was sitting up in bed, eating his dinner, so I sat beside him and chatted for a while. After a while Mammy came in to take his tray away.

As she walked out of the room he looked towards the door and asked, 'Who's that woman?'

I smiled and answered, 'That's your wife, Patsy.'

At the word 'wife' his head spun round to face me. '*My* wife? Am I married?' I nodded my head in response. He smiled and said in astonishment, 'God, she's a good-looking woman!' I laughed and told him I agreed. There was a moment's silence before he asked, 'And who are you?'

'I'm your daughter, Mary.'

'You're my daughter! Well, holy God!'

'Daddy, you have five children!' I reached up and took our family photo from its place on the wall and pointed out his three sons and two daughters.

'Three sons?! And two daughters?!' With that he started laughing, his shoulders bouncing up and down as his joy came out in great huffs and puffs. And then he suddenly asked, 'And where am I?'

'You're in the back downstairs room of your house.'

'*My* house? Do I own it?'

'Yes, Daddy,' I answered smiling.

'And what's outside this room?'

I described the house for him in detail. 'Well, there's the front room, the hallway, the kitchen, the back garden, and upstairs there's three bedrooms and a bathroom.'

His response to this was great surprise. 'A bathroom! Is there a bath in it?'

I couldn't hold in the laughter at that. 'Yes, Daddy, there's a big bath in it!'

'Ho ho! Well, holy God!'

When Shay and Michael came in that evening I told them about the conversation I'd had with Daddy. With that the two of them went into his room, hoisted him gently out of the bed and carried him in their arms in a fireman's lift around the house; he was light as a feather since his illness. It was as if he was being told his life story and he had never heard it before. It was heart-warming to see how amazed he was to hear about the life he had lived. He died three weeks later in the hospice in Harold's Cross, with all his family around him.

As the boat pulled in we saw that there was a big crowd there. All the islanders had gathered to welcome home one of its sons. The men of the island took turns carrying the coffin the hundred yards to the only graveyard on Rathlin; it was the resting place for

Protestants and Catholics alike on the island. The prayers were said quickly as the storm gathered around us and flowers were laid on Daddy's coffin as his children sang 'Amazing Grace'.

Everyone adjourned to the only pub on the island where we danced and sang and played until the early hours. The storm raged outside throughout the night but we were all happy that we had got Daddy back to the place where he always wanted to be.

Mammy was relieved too that the funeral was over and that Daddy was back in his beloved Rathlin.

When I woke the next morning I was pleased to see that the storm had passed and it was calm. I had to be down in Wexford that night to start a long tour of Ireland. As me, Joe and the boys got on the boat back to Ballycastle we noticed flower petals surrounding the boat. The petals were from flowers laid on Daddy's grave the day before. As the boat pulled away the flowers left a trail behind it. I always believed that that was Daddy's way of saying thanks and goodbye.

Those first few gigs after my dad died were tough. It was a strange feeling to go on stage and smile for the audience when I felt so sad inside. He had been sick for a while, which made things easier in a way because I didn't want him to suffer any more and I had prepared myself for his death. But I don't think you can truly prepare yourself for the death of a parent. It racked the bones of me even though I knew it was coming and his passing meant he was no longer suffering.

However, hard though it was, the show had to go on and with the success of *No Frontiers* the tours were becoming longer, more frequent and further afield.

Soon after the call from Bill Straw we got a similar call from a Mr Fujimoto from King Records in Tokyo. Eventually he too came to Dublin and we signed a deal for the release of *No Frontiers* in Japan.

King Records had decided to release a series of world music albums and *No Frontiers* was to be one of them. However, when they listened to the album again they felt that it would merit a proper release and promotion in its own right. Before we knew it, we were on our way to Tokyo for our first Japanese tour.

When we arrived at Narita Airport we were met by Yoko Nozaki, who worked for the label. She was a tiny girl who only came up to my shoulder (I'm only 5 feet 3). I remember thinking how young she looked (she was twenty at the time) with her little round glasses, a dark fringe and straight black hair that framed her face. She was a huge fan and started crying when she met us as she was so overjoyed.

Yoko looked after us for the whole trip and did so in a way that we had never experienced before. Every detail of the tour was meticulously mapped out. Nothing was left to chance, from the moment we got up every morning to the minute our heads hit the pillows at night; even the toilet breaks were accounted for!

I quickly found out that this was the Japanese way and it took us a while to get used to it.

The night of the first gig the venue was packed. I think it was about a 600-seater and we were to do two shows on the same night. We started into the concert and after each song there would be about five seconds of complete silence from the audience before they started to clap, very politely.

After a few songs I was beginning to get worried . . . did they not like us? In fact, I came off stage thinking they hated us or that we were crap, until, to my surprise, I heard them clapping for an encore.

The clapping had a kind of reverence about it and as I walked back on stage I saw they were all on their feet and many of them had tears streaming down their faces. Even when we were all back on stage the clapping continued. I looked around at the band and we just stared at each other in disbelief, shrugging our shoulders before we started into 'Another Day' as the applause endured.

After the show I went out to meet some fans and sign autographs as I usually did and could not believe the mass of people who were waiting for me. They were all very polite and waited their turn in line to meet me but it seemed like every second one was crying and telling me how moved they were by the show – and almost all of them had a present for me. They brought origami paper kits, flowers, ornaments, bottles of sake, even toys for my kids (most of them knew them by name)! Coming home from that trip I had to buy another suitcase for the gifts I'd received for the kids and myself. It was an amazing experience. They were delighted that I had come all the way to Japan to sing for them.

I was told later that the silence after each song and the polite applause was customary in Japan and a sign of respect as they didn't want to interrupt the atmosphere between songs.

While it was obvious to me from my experience with the audiences and my dealings with the record label staff that politeness was part of Japanese culture, to my surprise I discovered they really knew how to party when the work was done.

After the show the sake would flow like there was no tomorrow and the Japanese were well able to hold their own against us Irish. Every five minutes there would be a shout of 'Kanpai!' (which translates roughly to 'Bottoms up!' or 'Cheers!') and another shot would be downed. The next morning, however, the previous night's revelry would never be spoken of. While the band and myself would joke and laugh about the antics of the previous night, the Japanese would not engage in the banter. We noticed, too, that while we would all be nursing hangovers, they would never show theirs. It seemed that another Japanese custom was 'what happened after work stayed after work'!

I've always felt so lucky to do the job I love and at the same time get to experience new and different cultures and meet fascinating people around the world. I was to meet even more fascinating people on my next adventure.

In 1991 Philip King brought a group of Irish musicians to Nashville as part of a five-part television series. It would explore every aspect of Irish music as it travelled with its immigrants to America and it was called 'Bringing It All Back Home'. I was honoured to be included in this project with artists like Donal Lunny, Paul Brady, Emmylou Harris, Pete Seeger, U2, Dolores Keane, Sharon Shannon, The Everly Brothers, Hothouse Flowers, Richard Thompson and many others.

Philip's idea was to bring Irish music to America and create a meeting of Irish and American musicians. American music had been greatly influenced by Irish immigrants and this is evident today in American country, Appalachian, bluegrass and even Cajun music.

We spent a week in Nashville and recorded in a studio called Jack's Tracks; cowboy Jack Clement, a legendary figure in Nashville, owned it. Donal Lunny was the overall musical director and played on many of the sessions.

It was such an exciting trip for me as I got to sing alongside some amazing musicians, including Emmylou Harris and Richard Thompson. One of the highlights was doing two songs with Emmylou and Dolores Keane. We sang 'Sonny' and 'The Grey Funnel Line' in three-part harmony. Our voices blended really well together; with Dolores's rich, deep tones in the lower end, Emmylou doing a sweet high harmony and me some-where in the middle. It was such a thrill to meet Emmylou and get to know her over that week. We hit it off and found we had a lot in common. Our paths were to cross many times after that, when we would record and perform together over the years; some of the high-lights were projects such as the Transatlantic sessions in Scotland, a TV special in RTÉ for Irish and American television and a live concert filmed from the Kennedy Centre in Washington DC.

It was around this time that I was getting so much work I felt I had to take on someone to help mind the kids. Joe was getting busier too with the label and Mammy was getting older and I felt it was too much to ask her to take care of the three of them.

Janice L'estrange was the first person I interviewed

and I could tell she was really nervous. She was in her forties with short brown hair and glasses and had a lovely strong Dublin accent. She sat in my front room and handed me her one reference. It came from a local priest and it said she was a good and trustworthy person who loved children. When she saw Róisín, who was only three weeks old at the time, she nearly melted.

'Oh, I love babies,' she said. 'I've had six of my own.'

I wasn't used to interviewing people. I always minded my own kids when I could, so I was a bit awkward too. But Janice told me about her life and I was really drawn to her. This was the first job she had gone for as she had just split from her husband and she'd had a hard time of it.

Somehow my instincts told me that she was right for my family and I didn't interview anyone else. I told her there and then she could start the next Monday. I knew I was taking a chance but my intuition told me to go for it – and it proved to be one of the best decisions I ever made.

She would pick up the boys from school, make their dinner, light the fire. In fact, she did everything I would do if I was there myself. She loved my kids like her own, especially Róisín, who she spoilt rotten for the next fourteen years.

Most of Janice's own children were grown up by the

time she came to help me. Her youngest, David, was about ten at the time and he sometimes came with her to work when he was off school.

It was a weight lifted from my shoulders when touring got really hectic after the release of *No Frontiers*, as I knew the kids had Janice to take good care of them.

It was around this time too, that I found another great person to help out on the business side of things: Hazel Reynolds.

I first met Hazel in 1991 when I interviewed her to work in a beauty salon I was starting up in Rathmines. The salon was a project that I wanted to pursue for myself and I was looking for someone to run the day-to-day goings on of the business.

I got on with Hazel from the moment I met her. She was a really friendly, happy girl who was only twenty-three at the time. I always try to follow my hunches with the people I meet and with Hazel I just got this good feeling about her.

In the end, the project failed miserably, through no fault of Hazel's, so I decided to stick with the day job. However, I didn't want to lose Hazel. With things getting so busy with Joe and the record label, I suggested he take on Hazel as his assistant. She's now been working with us for twenty-three years. She's the one who works behind the scenes in the office and has become a close friend over the years. She takes great pride in every little success that the company or I have had, and with a broad smile, sparkling blue eyes and a fist held high in the air, is often heard to say, 'What a company!'

It's two o'clock in the morning and me and the band and crew are sitting around having a few drinks after the show in the Gleneagle Hotel in Killarney. Spirits are high as they often are after a gig, with adrenaline still pumping and a few drinks on board. Noel Brazil sits close by with a pint of Guinness in hand. We had enlisted him to be the support slot on that stretch of Irish shows in late 1990. Noel was ahead of the posse in the drinks stakes as he had come off stage an hour and a half before the rest of us, so he was pretty much steaming by this time.

He picked up his guitar at one stage, leaned across to me and said, 'I want you to listen to this song.'

> Babes in the wood, walking through snow,
> Big bad wolf at the window.
> Not much choice in the matter now,
> Some must lead some must follow . . .

The depth and passion that oozed out of Noel as he started singing stopped us all in our tracks. The entire bar fell silent. Though he sang in almost a whisper it was as if he was restraining an anger behind the words, holding himself back.

He turned to me as he finished and asked, 'Do you like it, Mary?' How could he not know from my expression that I loved it? It always meant so much to Noel when I recorded his songs and at that moment I knew that I had another Noel Brazil gem.

I first met Noel back in 1985 in The Meeting Place. Declan had said to me, 'You've got to come and see this guy, he's a remarkable writer.' In that short set he sang 'Ellis Island' and 'Columbus', and I was hooked. His lyrics had a depth and intensity that sucked you in from the very first line. As Declan described it, he had an 'emotional urgency' in his delivery that not everybody understood. I don't think he ever received the recognition he deserved both as a writer and a performer. Some people didn't rate him as a vocalist but I always thought no one could sing his songs better than he could.

Armed with some great songs from Irish writers Noel, Jimmy MacCarthy, Thom Moore and Kieran Goss, we set about the task of recording my fifth studio album, *Babes In The Wood*. In contrast to *No Frontiers*, there was harmony in the studio in terms of both the music and the relationships between the musicians. We recorded in Windmill Lane Studios on Ringsend Road with Andrew Boland engineering.

Declan, Pat, Garvan, Carl, Noel and myself had been

touring and working together as a band for a few years at this stage and had built up a musical understanding of one another. This made the process of recording run so much smoother and allowed for more free-flowing musical ideas and expression. Máire Breatnach played on the album too, on fiddle and synth. A gifted musician and writer from Dublin, she joined the band and was with us for the next few years.

The album was released in May 1991 and was my first album to go straight into the number-one spot. It stayed there for five weeks. We were all thrilled. Life at this stage was becoming a roller-coaster of recording, touring, TV and radio appearances. And being a mam to three kids as well meant I was never short of things to do. Looking back, I really don't know how I managed to juggle it all. It was an exciting time but it put me under a lot of pressure too. Following *Babes* we began a major tour of Ireland, starting with ten nights in the Olympia Theatre, Dublin.

Upon the release of the album I was offered a sponsorship deal by Alfa Romeo and they gave me a new sporty green car. It was the first day of the dates in the Olympia and I was due to pick up my brother Michael from the airport. Shay was already home and he came with Róisín and me for the trip.

It was mid-July and the sun was out but there had been a heavy rainfall that morning and the roads were still wet. When I was driving up Dorset Street I noticed Róisín in the back had got out of her car seat. I told her to get back in her seat quick but she was stubborn and wouldn't listen. Just then, when half my attention was in my rear-view mirror, the lights ahead turned yellow and the taxi in front of me stopped suddenly. There was an almighty crunch as I went straight into the back of him. Luckily Shay, who was in the front passenger seat, flung his arm back just in time to stop Róisín from flying between the two front seats and through the windscreen. I was so relieved that no one was hurt but I was quite shook by it. My new car was a write-off. I had only had it for a few days.

I arrived into the sound check later that afternoon still shaking at the thought of what might have happened. Alfa Romeo were very good about it. They gave me another car the following week.

The ten nights at the Olympia were a great success, a sell-out without a seat to be had even in the gods.

I remember back in the early days of The Black Family, the five of us would be standing in the wings in nervous silence, waiting to take our places on the stage. If it was a particularly important gig or for whatever reason we were more nervous than usual, just before we were about to walk on Michael would say, 'Ah sure, fuck them if they can't take a joke!' and the five of us would go on in fits of laughter.

Over the years it was a phrase that I carried with me on tour with my own band. When it was a particularly big show or a very important gig you could see there were more nerves than usual; the lads would pace the wings quietly or swing their hands and their shoulders trying to warm up their muscles, or I would tap my foot quickly though there was no music yet. That first night in the Olympia was just like that, so just as the lights dimmed I broke the ice by saying, 'Ah sure, fuck them if they can't take a joke!' And we all walked on stage laughing.

It was a silly phrase in a way, said for the exact purpose of calming everyone's nerves. But in a way, too, there was truth in it; if people didn't like you, there was nothing you could do about it so you might as well get out there and enjoy yourself anyway.

It's easy in this industry to get caught up in what people think of you, to concentrate only on the negative energy out there and that 'what if' mentality, rather than appreciating the positives in the moment.

I enjoyed every moment of those gigs. With my dad's death still on my mind I think that car accident brought about a moment of clarity after that initial period of fear and shock. Often you can find yourself running the treadmill of life, juggling a career and a growing family, carelessly allowing yourself to think that you and the ones you love are invincible. As I looked at Róisín asleep in bed that night I realized everything could change in an instant and I had to appreciate every moment, both in my family life and in my career.

As a friend of mine, Shane Howard, once said to me, 'These are the days that live.'

18

Great dreams and laid schemes

JOE KNEW PADDY Prendergast through a CD manu-facturing agency called A–Z Manufacturing where Paddy worked in London. He was from Waterford and first started working for them as a motorbike courier in his early twenties. He ended up making his way up the ladder and eventually bought the company from his boss when he retired.

After the success of *No Frontiers*, Paddy spoke to Joe about his plan of starting a new label in the UK and wanted me to be the flagship artist. Grapevine Records was born! I signed a licensing deal with Paddy and his partner Steve Ferney. I became the first release on Grapevine Records with *Babes In The Wood*. Up to 1991 we had exported CDs to the UK and now for the first time we had a proper release on a UK label that would get behind it.

Paddy had the look of John Lennon about him, with his round glasses and his fair hair. He had a real appetite for business and success with a great sense of humour too; he was always up for a bit of craic after the gigs. Paddy and Steve did a great job promoting the album and quickly built up a career for me in the UK.

I did numerous promotional tours with Pat and Declan around Britain but I have to admit, it was a hard slog; I was going from a country where I was famous to a country where I was relatively unknown. So we had a lot of ground to cover in order to get a foothold in this new market and we'd travel hundreds of miles every day to get to different radio or TV stations, like *The Terry Wogan Show*, BBC Radio 1 and all the regional BBCs – sometimes seven or eight stations in one day.

Paddy and Steve were really building Grapevine from the bottom up so in the early days Steve would double up as a driver on promotional tours. He came from Sunderland and, like Paddy, he had a great sense of humour. He was a little older than Paddy and had a strong northern English accent, which I really loved. He recalled a story on one of those early trips to me recently.

We had had a long gruelling day of interviews and travelling and we were all dying to get some grub into us. Pat had his accordion with him and wanted to leave it behind reception rather than drag it all the way back up to the hotel room before we went out to eat. The receptionist looked at this enormous black box, the accordion case, and asked, 'What is it?'

'Well, it's an instrument,' Pat replied but still she looked confused. 'It's an accordion.'

With his quick wit Declan piped up, 'Will you make up your mind, Pat!'

We all fell about the place laughing. Steve too, he loved the quick wit and banter that we had together and quickly fell into the repartee.

Paddy and Steve did a great job of getting my name out in the UK and I started to build up a strong following. The two of them quickly became part of the Mary Black adventure, helping to further the project while at the same time becoming part of the tour family. Paddy eventually became my manager in the UK and opened up various opportunities around Europe for me as well. They did licensing deals with record companies in Holland, Germany and Scandinavia and before long we began to tour these countries.

After recording *Babes In The Wood*, Máire Breatnach wanted to pursue her own career in writing and producing and recommended a friend of hers, Eleanor McEvoy, to replace her in the band. Eleanor was also a classically trained violinist who played keyboards and sang. She was just twenty-five years old when I first met her. She had her own distinct style and personality; her dark hair was short on one side and long on the other, and she always wore her trademark silver ear cuff that stretched halfway across her cheek. She was a songwriter, too, and had her own band. I always enjoyed having another woman in the band, especially when we were on the road. It was a different dynamic than when it was just the lads and me.

Around this time Joe and his brother Paul had an idea to bring out a compilation album of artists who were on the Dara label. With the label as small as it was they were a little short on tracks so they decided to license a few songs from other artists for the album.

As they pursued this idea they found that a strong female presence was evolving. It seemed at the time that there was a real strength in successful female artists in Ireland: Maura O'Connell, Dolores Keane, Sharon Shannon, and my sister Frances, who had just released a very successful album with Kieran Goss. I remember suggesting to Joe that maybe we should make it an all-female album and coincidentally a friend of Paul's, Michael Croke from RTÉ Commercial Enterprises, suggested the same thing to Paul. So Joe went about compiling the songs while restricting it to female artists. The plan was to confine it to six women with two tracks from each one.

At this stage Eleanor had been in the band for a couple of months and I had been listening to her singing her own songs backstage after shows. In her rich deep voice she sang each of her songs with great emotion.

I remember being extremely moved by one song in particular. It was called 'Only A Woman's Heart'. When Joe was choosing the various tracks I suggested that Eleanor should be on the album singing this song as I felt that it was so poignant and relevant to the overall feel of the album.

Paul resisted this idea at first as he felt the album was for established artists rather than unrecorded new-comers. I felt so strongly about it that I suggested then that Eleanor and I could sing the song together. They went for it, and soon after, we went into the studio to record it. It was a move that would become pivotal to the success of the album. 'Only A Woman's Heart' was the only song recorded especially for the project; we were very happy with how it turned out and it seemed the obvious choice for the title track.

The single 'Only A Woman's Heart' was quietly released with minimal advertisement in July 1992; there were no high expectations for it, Joe and Paul just thought the album would be a good project for the label. Within weeks, however, radio picked up on it and started playing it with fervour.

This exposure gave the album a huge boost when it came out that August and its momentum just kept on building. It went to number one quite quickly and we thought it would fizzle out soon after that. We were wrong; it held the number-one spot that

Christmas – a full four months after its first release.

Steve Ferney said that Universal in England were calling their Dublin office asking why *The Bodyguard* soundtrack wasn't number one in Ireland that Christmas when it was number one in almost every other country in the world. Selling over 750,000 units, *A Woman's Heart* went on to become the bestselling album in Irish chart history.

It was a great achievement for a small independent label but I don't think at the time any of us realized the significance of it. All of the artists involved benefited significantly and not just financially. The album gave their careers a terrific boost. The only downside for me was that through *A Woman's Heart* I lost a great musician in Eleanor, who went on to pursue her solo career.

In September 1992 the single had really taken off and Tom Zuta happened to be visiting Ireland from LA. He was an A&R man (a talent scout) from Geffen Records. This record label from California was a subsidiary of Universal Music Group and had artists like Joni Mitchell, Rufus Wainwright and Neil Young on its roster. While travelling through Dublin he heard 'Only A Woman's Heart' on the radio and asked the limo driver who was singing.

'That's Eleanor McEvoy,' he told him. 'She's playing in the Baggot Inn tonight.' Zuta went down to Eleanor's show that evening and more or less signed her on the spot. I was so happy for Eleanor. It was a well-deserved break for her, but all the same I was sad to lose her.

I made my film debut a short time after the release of *A Woman's Heart*. A director called Dudi Appleton got in touch saying he was coming to one of my shows in the Ulster Hall in Belfast and wanted to talk to me about a film he was making. Dudi had a lovely personality and I immediately liked him when I met him after the show that night. He told me he had a part in his film that he thought would be perfect for me.

I laughed out loud when he said that and replied, 'Sure, I've never acted in my life.'

He smiled and said, 'No, honestly, I think you'll be perfect.' I told him I'd think about it and over the following few weeks he contacted me numerous times and was very persuasive until eventually I agreed to do it.

It was a short film called *A Sort of Homecoming* and it was set in the countryside in County Down. I played the mother of Robby, a sixteen-year-old boy who has just returned home from a youth detention centre. The story continues as he gradually begins to unravel the passion and betrayal that had given him his identity.

Getting to do something I had never done before was an interesting experience for me. Singing a song and learning the words of it was one thing, but acting out lines was another and I found it quite difficult. However,

Dudi seemed happy with my performance. In a few scenes I had to be sitting smoking a cigarette, looking worried. They knew I didn't smoke any more so they offered me a herbal cigarette, to which I said, 'No, if I have to smoke I'm going to smoke a real cigarette and enjoy it . . . I'll do it for my art!' There were a few takes so there were two cigarettes smoked. When Dudi shouted 'Cut', I still had half a cigarette left, which they tried to take off me, but I decided I'd started it so I'd better finish it. It was the last cigarette I ever smoked.

About five years later Dudi cast me in a small part in *The Most Fertile Man in Ireland*. That was the extent of my acting career!

It was late in 1992 that the promoter John Nicholls brought me and the band out to tour Australia. Back then Australia had a policy that international acts had to have an Australian support act when touring the country. I thought this was a great policy as it promoted the country's local music in an industry dominated by British and American acts. John suggested a well-known singer/songwriter from Warrnambool in Victoria, Shane Howard, to open the show.

Shane had strong Irish roots and a keen interest in Irish music. He had had great success with a band called Goanna in the 1980s and went on to have a thriving solo career. It proved to be a fortuitous meeting. I had toured

Australia before as a special guest with The Chieftains and I loved it. I loved the Australian people I met and found them to be open-minded and intelligent with a great love of music. Coming from Ireland in winter, Australia seemed to have great light and colour and the sun seemed to always shine. Shane and his musicians, Tim Wedde (piano) and Bill Jacobi (bass), were so much fun to be around, I'll always remember that trip.

The tour took us to most of the major cities in Australia and New Zealand and over the course of the trip Shane and I became good friends. I was really taken by his songs; so much so that I brought home with me from that tour a new song of his called 'Flesh and Blood'. It would be the first single from my 1993 album *The Holy Ground* and the first of the many songs of Shane's that I would record.

We invited Shane over to do support for me on *The Holy Ground* tour the following May. He arrived at Dublin Airport and was picked up by my good friend Pat Armstrong. A few minutes into the journey 'Flesh and Blood' was blaring out of the car speakers.

Shane asked Pat, 'Is that the new Mary Black album you have there?'

'No, no,' he replied, 'that's the new single on the radio.' Shane was gobsmacked; he couldn't believe he was listening to one of his own songs on Irish radio!

The Holy Ground album went platinum on the day of

its release and was followed by the biggest Irish tour I ever did. It included five nights in the Point Depot in Dublin, five nights in the Opera House in Cork, and four nights in UCL, Limerick, as well as gigs in Waterford, Galway, Belfast, Wexford, Killarney and more.

They were such happy times. We had so much fun on the road, the band, the crew and myself. Along with Declan, Pat, Carl and Garvan we had added Dave Early on drums and Frank Gallagher on fiddle and synth. The crew at that point was Damian McCollum (tour manager), Billy Robinson (front of house/sound), Paul 'Minnie' Moore (monitors), Liam McCarthy (lights), Trevor Plunkett (backline roadie) and Maeve Kearney (hairdresser and PA).

Maeve used to work in a hairdresser's off Grafton Street called Cat's, where I would go to get my hair cut. I loved the way she did my hair and we got on really well. She was twenty-five at the time and I was thirty-seven, but even with the age difference we just clicked and it didn't take me long to ask her if she wanted to come on tour as my hairdresser and PA. I was touring a lot then and never felt I could manage my frizzy hair when I was on the road.

As well as that I missed having a woman on tour after Eleanor left. It seems to me that all my life I've always felt like a bit of a tomboy, just one of the lads. I never had a big problem with being the only girl on tour; I loved the laddish banter and could always hold my own with the guys in the band and crew. At the same time, though, I was a girl and it could get lonely sometimes without another girl on tour.

Fortunately, Maeve jumped at the chance to join me and ended up touring with me for over ten years. Carl christened us 'Morag and Maude': two old inseparable biddies, always yapping and never out of each other's company. We're still great friends to this day.

It's hard to describe the craic we all had on tour. As I get older the tour stories escape me more and more, but in general we seemed always to be laughing. The dynamic between Carl, Dave and Trevor was one that you might see between three fifteen-year-old boys; constant messing and slagging and telling rude jokes, they always had the rest of us in fits of laughter.

Shane once said of Carl, 'For someone whose playing is like the voice of an angel, he has the mouth of a sewer!'

During *The Holy Ground* tour, after the fifth night in the Cork Opera House, a session started up in the bar of the Silver Springs Hotel where we were staying. All the band and crew were there as well as Shane and some other local musicians and friends. That night was the first time I met Seamus Begley. He was a well-known traditional singer, an accordion player and a farmer, from west Kerry. Within five minutes of meeting him it was evident that he was as mad as a hatter, trick-acting and joking to beat the band. He was a big handsome Kerry man with an enormous presence who could put you at ease and make you feel like you'd known him for years.

On this evening, as the hours passed, there was great singing, laughter and dancing. The tunes started up and after a while Seamus and Garvan got up and started half set-dancing and half trick-acting around the room. We were all in the upstairs lounge of the hotel, which was quite a long room and had full-length windows at one end that looked out on to the street.

We were gathered near the windows when Seamus and Garvan got up to dance and they took advantage of the full length of the lounge. The tune seemed to get faster as they danced and was adding to the madness of the scene. Once they got to the other end of the room they turned back towards us in a tango stance, their cheeks touching and their hands clasped together pointing at us. With that they started running full flight towards us. With each step they gained momentum and I looked on in horror as they approached, realizing that they were charging straight for the floor-length glass window. At the last second Garvan veered to the left and the two of them landed on a glass table instead, smashing it to pieces. We all roared with laughter, the two lads included, and there was a huge cheer and a big round of applause.

Seamus got up and came to sit beside me but as his

bum hit the chair he winced, 'Jesus! Me arse is killing me.' As he reached around to put his hand on it he pulled out a shard of glass. He still has the scar to this day, which he'd be happy to show anyone at the drop of a hat.

I'd often tell people that the hardest thing about life on the road is the time lost with family and friends at home. Of course, though, there is the other side of the coin. Apart from getting to do the job I love doing and getting to travel to new places, being on the road allows you to meet people that you would never have crossed paths with otherwise, people from different backgrounds, from different countries and different cultures. I've met some of the most extraordinary people on the road, whether they were fans or other musicians or just people I've come across along the way. Some have become lifelong friends; others have left a lasting impression on me after just one meeting. Whatever the circumstance, I feel I am a better person for having met them.

19

And there's peace in a travelling heart

IT WAS AT the highest point of my career that I found myself at my lowest. Tours were selling out worldwide, the phone never stopped ringing with interviewers and offers of work, and I had become a household name in Ireland.

My home life was just as good. The kids were happy and healthy, all was fine with me and Joe and we were more than financially stable. In fact, I had everything I'd ever wanted.

It's hard to describe the course that leads a person into depression. For me you might think: she had a beautiful, happy family, she did what she loved doing, she had a high-flying career – what was there to be depressed about? But for some people it's not that easy. Sometimes a seed can be planted in your mind and it takes root there, growing larger and larger until it engulfs your every thought. This is how it happened with me.

As my career grew, every achievement surprised and delighted me more and more. I never expected it to be as successful as it was. But as it grew so did the seed of doubt. 'Am I as good as they think I am? Do I deserve this?' These were some of the questions that I started to ask myself more and more.

Around the same time I also began to feel that Declan was becoming unhappy in the band and with the work that we were doing.

In late 1994 we started recording my seventh album, *Circus*, in Windmill Lane Studios, but to me there just didn't seem to be the same enthusiasm from Declan as there once was. Although he threw himself into producing and playing with commitment, I felt his hunger for it was waning and because of the way I was feeling I began to think that this was somehow because of me and I was to blame.

These negative thoughts slowly trickled into my live performances. While I'm sure it affected my singing a little bit, I knew I could pull that off. But the introductions and chat between songs became more difficult for me. I felt Declan thought my introductions were stupid, that I was stupid, that I had nothing interesting to say, and so I began to speak less and less on stage. It wasn't that Declan ever said anything like this, it was just how I felt at the time.

It got to the point where I would give the minimal

amount of information about a song, which would be rehearsed in my head beforehand. This was something I never wanted to do as a performer; I always wanted to be natural and true to the audience and give something of myself as I chatted to them. My anxiety didn't allow that. There was no spontaneity or true warmth, although I doubt the audience noticed as I smiled through it all.

When the anxiety and fear trickled into my everyday life I knew I had a problem. I went around feeling I had nothing interesting to say so I began to talk less and less at home. My zest for life had faded as my self-confidence weakened. I had to do something. Having been depressed before, I could see where this was going and had the foresight to get help. The dark days I had with post-natal depression were all too memorable and I feared they might come again.

I visited my doctor and he immediately put me on anti-depressants.

We were somewhere in Belgium on the tour bus when Declan asked to speak to me privately. It was early 1995 and we had taken a break from recording to do a two-week tour of Belgium, Holland and Germany with the intention of finishing recording *Circus* when we got home.

The tour bus was a double-decker with bunks on the upper level and two living areas downstairs. Declan and I walked into the back lounge area and sat down. I was curious as to what he wanted to talk about and didn't really have an inkling about what he was going to say.

I could see from his expression that it was something serious and he seemed to pick his words carefully. He told me he was going to leave the band; he wanted to work with other people and explore other types of music. He felt he'd come as far as he could with our partnership and the time was right for him to move on to other projects. At the time he was producing Sinéad Lohan and was interested in gigging with her.

At first I didn't know what to say. My initial reaction was panic and fear because while other members of the band came and went there was always that strong unit of me and Dec that could cope with whatever was thrown at us. Now Declan was leaving. Even though I was shocked that he was saying this, in my heart I wasn't that surprised.

'Well, if that's how you feel, that's what you have to do,' I said eventually. I waffled on for a while about different things, I think trying to deflect the emotions that were building inside me.

It was around this time also that Joe and I had been thinking of having another baby and we knew that if we were going do it, it had to be sooner rather than later as I was nearly forty. I mentioned this to Declan, and he thought it was a great idea.

'That'd be brilliant!' he said. I think he felt the

timing would be good all round – him leaving coinciding with me taking time out to have a baby. I think he also felt guilty about leaving me because perhaps he felt that his input was so crucial to the partnership and it would fall apart without him. He didn't feel so bad now that I was planning for baby number four.

After we talked for a while we hugged and he told me he'd finish the work on *Circus* and the tour that he'd committed to in the US that March. I felt very strange when I went back to my bunk. I guess I couldn't quite believe what I'd just heard. I couldn't sleep thinking about the future and what was ahead of me.

While I was lying there considering the prospect of giving up singing, I had a Eureka moment. I thought, 'Hang on a second!' I literally sat up in my bed. 'You were singing long before you met Declan, and you'll be singing long after he's gone.' I knew then that it wasn't over. Things began to make sense. I didn't realize at the time how difficult working together had become for us. Neither of us seemed to be happy, and I knew then the best thing for both of us was to go our separate ways. Once I understood this, the relief was immense; I began to feel better from that moment on.

After the gig the following night we called a meeting for the band. Declan and I decided we'd tell them all together. I looked around the room at the men who had become such a big part of my life: Pat, Carl, Garvan,

Dave, Frank and Declan, and I couldn't help but wonder if this was the end of an era. I could tell the band were nervous; we rarely had heavy band talks. When we sat around a big table in the green room, they knew it was serious. Declan spoke and told them our news. There was total silence for what seemed like an age. Nobody knew what to say.

Afterwards, there was hand-shaking and back-slapping and some nice things said, but somehow I felt there was a sense of relief for the band, too. During the rest of the tour it was like a weight had been lifted from us and we all got on really well; Declan was in great form.

I knew I had a huge mountain to climb to find some-one to fill Declan's shoes, but I also felt at this stage in my career I had the tools to find someone great and that I was ready to become a leader myself.

That night taught me a lot about myself. I could have fallen down under the weight of doing this on my own, but I found out that I had a fire inside me, that I was much stronger than I ever thought I was and my passion for singing and performing was much more powerful than my fear of going it alone. I felt that passion burn bright for the first time in a long time.

We went home and finished *Circus* without a hitch. I think we all made the most of that recording session, knowing it would be our last together. The same went for our final tour together in the States that March.

Our last show was in the Symphony Hall in Boston and I came off the stage with so many emotions running through me at the same time. I was sad that Declan was leaving, the memories of our journey together came flooding back, but at the same time I was excited at the prospect of a new path and a new adventure.

After the show I made a speech to the band and crew, thanked Declan for his contribution over the years and gave him a little present.

Our hotel was around the corner from a tiny pub called the Littlest Bar, owned by a lovely Mayo man called Paddy Grace. It probably only held about twenty people, which was just enough for our party.

At the pub Declan and I sat together talking until about five in the morning. We talked about everything: life, music, love, loss.

As we walked home together, my arm linking his, he said to me, 'That was the best chat I think we've ever had.' And we both threw our heads back laughing. Funny that we left it to the last moment to have it.

After that tour we needed a guitar player as soon as possible. *Circus* was to be launched that summer and we already had gigs booked to promote it. Bill Shanley had been playing in Eleanor's band and had heard through the grapevine that Declan was leaving. He called Joe and put his name forward for the position.

I knew Bill from recording the song 'Only A Woman's Heart', and I was aware that he was a really good guitar player. However, I was concerned by the fact that he was only twenty-three at the time and lacked experience at our level. I told him to listen to half a dozen of our songs and we'd meet up a week later to have a run through and we'd see how this went.

The following week Pat came up from Kinsale to join us, and the three of us sat in the front room of my house and played for an hour or so. Bill, who was from Clonakilty, was tall and thin with a dark Afro-style hair-cut and he had a calm, gentle demeanour. The session felt good, Bill had obviously done his homework. He impressed me even more by what he said when he was leaving: 'Mary, I know I can make this work and I'm willing to work very hard to make it happen.'

I believed him and I decided to give him a shot. I knew it was going to be really difficult to fill Declan's shoes, and I gave Bill about twenty-five songs to learn from the new album and from the back catalogue. He had eight weeks to learn them. I found out later that he spent those eight weeks in a bedsit in Dublin doing nothing but playing the guitar and fine-tuning the songs.

Our first gig together was in the Mean Fiddler on Wexford Street in Dublin (now The Village). It was a benefit gig for Women's Aid. It went well and I was happy. It was different, which I expected it to be, but I could see the potential.

We launched *Circus* on a beautiful hot August day in the grounds of St Audeon's Church near Christ Church Cathedral in Dublin. We went all out with the circus theme, with a circus tent, jugglers, clowns on stilts and fire breathers. It was very much a family affair with all our families and friends joining us as well as the press and colleagues.

It was a happy day with lots of laughter. We performed some of the songs from the new album with Bill at the helm and I began to feel confident and excited about the next chapter of my life. Bill was doing a great job and often turned to me for direction. This allowed me to be more creative as I knew how I wanted the songs to come across and I was able to convey that to Bill and know that he was listening. It was very empowering. I felt I had a voice again and it was worthy of being heard.

20

Caught between the settled life and on the road again

I THINK IT was Joe who took the call that day in early 1995; it was a normal day. He'd walked in the door that evening and I was in the kitchen making dinner. As he picked up Róisín and gave her a kiss hello, he turned to me and said, 'Joan Baez's offices were on the phone today; they were looking for you. She has a project she wants to talk to you about.'

I was very excited. 'Joan Baez? I love Joan Baez!' I'd been listening to her music since I was a kid. The first song I ever learnt on guitar was one of her songs, 'Dona, Dona, Dona'. I was a folkie even at that age and loved the tone of her voice and the songs she sang. Though we didn't have any of her records (because we had no record player), I would tune into BBC Radio Scotland or Radio 4 and we would catch her on folk programmes.

I kept asking Joe questions: 'What did they say? What's the project? Did you talk to Joan herself? What did they say *exactly*?!' But Joe just smiled and shrugged his shoulders. 'I don't know, Mary, they just wanted your number so she could call you personally.' I was chuffed at the prospect of getting a call from *the* Joan Baez.

It was lunchtime the next day when the phone rang. I answered and heard a soft American accent ask, 'Hi, is that Mary? It's Joan here, Joan Baez.' She started off by telling me how much she enjoyed my music and had many of my albums. She explained that she had this idea to do a live album from the Bottom Line in New York. The Bottom Line was a famous venue in Greenwich Village in Manhattan, a great live club, and down through the years so many great musicians from jazz to folk to blues and country had gigged there. I had played there myself in the 1980s with De Dannan when we toured America. Joan's idea was to invite all the female artists that she admired from different places and genres of music to join her on stage over a few nights.

Joan asked if I would be interested in being one of the guests. Of course, I jumped at the offer and was very flattered that she wanted to include me alongside names like Janis Ian, Mary Chapin Carpenter and The Indigo Girls, to name a few.

We started to talk about songs and she immediately said she wanted me to sing 'Song For Ireland'. She then suggested we do something more traditional, such as 'She Moves Through The Fair' or 'Carrick Fergus'. I couldn't get enthusiastic about those suggestions because while they were beautiful songs they had been covered by so many people over the years.

It was Joe who had the idea that it would be great to do a Dylan song, seeing as she had such a close connection with Dylan in the early days. We had been listening to 'Oh Mercy' and particularly liked the song 'Ring Them Bells' from that album. I suggested this to Joan and she kind of liked the idea and seemed willing to consider it. I knew I would be bringing Pat, my piano player, as we had already decided on 'Song For Ireland', and that was one song I did with just him, so I thought he could work out a nice version of 'Ring Them Bells' on piano, too.

There was the odd phone call back and forth between us over the following weeks but there would be no time for rehearsal; we just couldn't get together until I went over for the show. Obviously, this wasn't ideal, but I was confident that it would all work out fine.

Within weeks I was on my way to New York and when we arrived at the Bottom Line for the sound check there were already people queuing out the door.

Joan was on stage when we walked in but as soon as she saw me she jumped down off the stage and gave me a big hug. I was surprised at how beautiful she was in real life. Big brown eyes, high cheekbones, white teeth, beautiful olive skin and no make-up. She welcomed me warmly.

The sound check was our first meeting and our only rehearsal for the show that was on that night. We worked through 'Ring Them Bells', and though we were on a tight schedule, it went well. Pat had come up with a beautiful arrangement on the piano that was quite different from the original and Joan was impressed.

When we finished 'Ring Them Bells', for my own peace of mind I needed to quickly run over 'Song For Ireland'. As I did, Joan sat at the edge of the stage and listened. Halfway through the last verse I looked over at her and she was crying, tears were streaming down her face.

When we got on stage together that night we didn't quite stick to what we did in rehearsal. There were added 'oh's and 'ah's and there were places we came in that hadn't been planned, but it was what came naturally to us, and even though it wasn't perfect, we caught the atmosphere of the night and it was heartfelt. I totally nailed them with 'Song For Ireland' afterwards! It's always very moving to see people's reaction when I sing that song.

The project as a whole was a great success; the audiences loved the concept and the music. Joan decided to call the album *Ring Them Bells*, which I thought was very appropriate considering all the lovely belles that sang on it.

Joan also loved to sketch and I remember before we

left she handed me a drawing. It had been quickly drawn but it was an adept caricature she must have done after the sound check. It showed me singing on stage with Pat at the piano, and her sitting at the side of the stage, her little plait hanging around her shoulder and tears bursting out of her eyes as a bubble came out of my mouth that read, '. . . and I sang a song for Ireland.'

When I got home from that short trip to New York I only had a few precious days to spend with my kids before I embarked on a 25-date whistle-stop tour of the UK. It would be one of the longest tours of my career, spanning almost five weeks (with a short break in the middle) and ending in three nights at London's Hammersmith Apollo. As usual I left home with a heavy heart, feeling the guilt of having to leave my children yet again.

I'm sitting on a sleeper bus staring out of the window as the rainy green landscape of England passes me by. I've been on the road for about two weeks now and thoughts of home have caught me in a quiet moment. I'm sitting on my own; the rest of the band and crew are watching a movie down the back or catching a few extra minutes of sleep in their bunks. That's when it hits me: I want to go home, I *really* want to go home.

I had been on the phone to Joe that morning, just before I got on the bus. The gig the night before in

Liverpool had been great but the subject of Danny and 'the game' had taken up most of our conversation.

Danny had just turned ten years old and was in fourth class in St Joseph's in Terenure. At that age he loved music but his real passion was Gaelic football. Joe was his coach at Templeogue GAA club where he played for the under-elevens, but he also played for his school's junior team in midfield. Gaelic football was and still is a big deal in our family; we were all huge supporters. Joe played and coached, Conor played, Danny played and Róisín played when she got older. As for me, I was the proud mother, always cheering them on from the sidelines.

That year Danny's school team had made it to the North and South Dublin Schools final, which was to be played in Croke Park against Scoil Mhuire, Marino. This was a big deal for Danny but, as was often the case, this important event clashed with one of my gigs. The game was coming up in a few days, just when I would be singing in Newcastle.

When Danny came on the phone that morning he was absolutely beside himself with excitement in antici-pation of the game. In his deep voice and with a slight lisp he told me all about the tough training regime they'd had that week and the pep talk their coach had given them at the end of the session. The coach had taken Danny aside and told him that because he scored two goals and four points in the semi-final, he wanted him to be captain for the final. As the captain, Danny would be the leader on the big day.

I could hear in his voice as he talked that he was jumping around in excitement, something he always did as a child. It later became a running joke in the family, especially when we were all together on holiday, that Danny's way of bouncing around would soon result in some minor accident. We used to tease him about it by taking bets on how long it would take for Danny to knock something over at the dinner table. It was usually in the first fifteen minutes.

As happy as I should have been for him in that moment, hearing his excited voice on the other end of the phone only made me more upset; once again I was missing a big moment in one of my children's lives.

Two years before this I had missed Conor's confirm-ation. I was on tour in Australia, which had been organized a year in advance, and it was all signed off and sealed by the time we found out when Conor's confirm-ation was taking place. Frances, who has a great relationship with all my kids, is Conor's godmother, so I asked her if she would stand in and be Conor's 'Mammy' for the day. I had stepped in for her at Eoghan's confirmation the year before when she was on tour. Joe was there too, of course, and my mother, along with lots of Conor's cousins. In fact, everyone was there except me. It hurt. It had been a big deal for Conor and I wasn't there. Those were the times when the guilt would kick in. 'What the hell am I doing here? I should be home with my family.' The kids were always very good about it, and they said they didn't mind, but I knew it would mean a lot to them if I was there on days like that, and it would have meant a lot to me, too. Now it was about to happen again, on a really important day for my son.

When I said my goodbyes down the phone to Danny, I told him how great I knew he was going to be, wished him luck and promised I'd call again before the game.

But as I sat on the bus looking out the window thinking about the conversation I'd just had, I started to feel angry that I couldn't promise him I was going to be there on his big day. I decided there and then that I was going to try my very best to get home, even though it didn't seem possible.

When I got off the bus at our next venue in Manchester I called Joe again. 'Joe, I really want to come home for Danny's match. Do you think you could look into a flight that would get me over and back in the same day in time for the gig in Newcastle?' Joe went to work and found just that. A same-day return that would get me back an hour before I had to be on stage. The next hurdle was Damian.

My tour manager of six years, Damian, ran a tight ship. He had everything on tour off to a T and left nothing to chance, especially when it came to making sure we were all in the right place at the right time. I knew he wasn't going to like it; if something went wrong with flights, or if I was late to the airport there was a big possibility I could miss the gig, something that had never happened before, but I had to talk to him about it.

Damian knew me well at that stage and he could tell I was upset when I walked into the production room. I told him how I felt, how I thought that as a mother it was really important that I be there for Danny; I needed to share the day with my son. I talked for a while and ended by asking him, 'If there was any way I could get back for a few hours to see the game, how would you feel about me going home?'

I could tell from Damian's expression it wasn't the best news he'd heard all day; I could see the thoughts of me missing the gig rise to the forefront of his mind. But he knew I'd made up my mind. And in reality he had no choice in the matter!

I told Joe not to tell Danny I was coming home; I wanted it to be a surprise. I was up at the crack of dawn for the flight to Dublin and Joe collected me from the airport. I was so happy to be home. We went straight to the match in Croke Park. The excitement in the crowd was electric. All the children from both schools had been bussed in for the big occasion and most of the players' families were there too. I was so proud when I saw Danny lead his team out of the tunnel, and I knew at that moment that whatever happened, whether they won or lost, I'd never regret coming.

St Joseph's won well and when Danny walked his team up to the podium to receive their trophy I'll never forget how he grabbed the cup and threw it up over his head like he had just won the All Ireland Final for Dublin. Even the trophy presenter looked at the crowd like, 'Wow, this kid's a pro at raising a trophy!' In that moment I was filled with such a huge sense of pride. Danny spotted me in the crowd as he was going up to collect the cup and I could tell he was thrilled I was there to share this big day with him. For all the achievements he's had since then, even now I look back and remember that day with such pride. I was so glad that I'd really pushed to make the trip. That precious memory was worth so much to me, and it still is today.

When I arrived back at the venue in Newcastle all was quiet and the place was deserted. The sound check was over and everyone had gone out to dinner. There was about an hour until show time so I went to my dressing room to relax.

Damian had told me to call him when I arrived back or, of course, if I had any problems on my travels. So I picked up the phone and decided to give him the fright of his life. He answered the phone and in a very distressed tone I said, 'Oh, Damian, I'm still in Dublin airport, the flight has been cancelled!'

There was a silence at the other end but I could feel the panic down the line. The crowds were streaming in . . . what was he going to do? Eventually he said, 'What?!'

I let it sit for a few seconds before I answered, '. . . Ah, I'm only messin'! I'm backstage.' Needless to say he had a conniption on the other end of the phone. To this day I don't think he's ever forgiven me – or been as happy to see me walk out on stage.

21

'Who Knows Where the Time Goes'

IT WAS UNUSUAL for me to tour with another artist, but when I was asked to do a double-bill tour with Janis Ian I jumped at the chance. I had been a big fan of hers since I first heard 'At Seventeen' in my late teens. By 1995 my popularity in Holland had grown greatly, but I was still doing smaller venues in Germany; Janis's situation was the opposite. It made sense that she would headline the shows in Germany and I would headline the shows in the Netherlands and in this way we would both reach a wider audience.

I met Janis for the first time at our first gig together in Utrecht in the Netherlands in early 1996. She was a tiny little woman, a good few inches smaller than me, and very polite. But after spending a little time with her I could see she was stressed. I think the problem was she was anxious to make sure that the stage managers and promoters treated her properly. In fact, she was a little stand-offish with the band and me for the first day or two of the tour.

Gradually, she relaxed and became more comfortable with us; she started to come out of her shell and was much more at ease around us. She loved the banter that I had with the band and the crew and she became part of it. I found out later that she had been hurt and treated badly by a lot of so-called friends in the music industry during her career. Because of this I think she had become cautious of people in the business. In my career I was lucky in that respect; while there had been ups and downs I'd never been badly stung. With Joe as my record label, manager and husband I was protected from the sharks that many other artists came across. It explained Janis's initial reticence and cautious manner towards us.

That night in Utrecht was also when I met Mark Van Setten for the first time. Mark, who had been a fan of mine for some years, was very young, extremely tall with dark hair and glasses. He was kind of shy, but passionate about the music, and he approached me that night with an offer. He told me that he'd realized there was no official Mary Black website and he offered to create one for me. This sounded like a great opportunity and I gladly accepted his offer. This was at the beginning of the internet phenomenon and Mark did an amazing job, creating a site that was quite ahead of its time. He's still our webmaster to this day and is constantly updating and developing the site. He is a fan who became a great friend over the years.

My daughter Róisín joined us for about a week on that tour. At that stage the tours were better organized, the places we stayed in were nicer, and I could afford to fly Róisín in and out for a few days. Being the only girl and the youngest in the family, she missed me a lot. I always felt guilty leaving her and now that I had the means to take her with me she often came on tour. She was only about seven then so I didn't mind taking her out of school. I felt that the places she got to see and the experiences she had while she was away with me were more valuable to her than a week of primary school education. She loved the band, the crew and the tour bus, and she got on like a house on fire with Janis when they met.

Every night Janis and I sang together at the end of the show and the tour was a great success. The most precious thing that I gained from that tour was Janis's friendship. We still are friends and keep in touch to this day. She wrote me a really nice letter, dated 9 May 1996, part of which read:

> I hope all is well with you and your brood and Joe
> isn't working too hard. If you see any of the boys
> [the band], give them my best. You are certainly one

of the nicest group of people I have ever toured
with, if not the nicest.

Janis sent me a copy of a compilation album that she
released in 1998 of unreleased songs called *Unreleased 1:
Mary's Eyes*. She explained that the title track was about me
and a moment she remembered on the tour. I recall it well.

I was on the tour bus and I was sitting with Róisín,
helping her with her homework as we travelled to the
next city. The subject was history, the topic was the Irish
famine. Janis was taken by the passion with which I
explained Irish history to my daughter. This, and listening to me sing songs like 'Song For Ireland', inspired her
to write this song:

> *Mary's eyes are startling blue*
> *and her hair's Newcastle gold*
> *and she walks the thin white line*
> *between the body and the soul*
>
> *She's as faithful to her history*
> *as a novice to his fast*
> *for she is standing on the bones of Ireland's past*
> *she is singing of the Troubles*
> *and a fire in the land*
> *'til I can almost feel the famine*
> *slipping through my trembling hand*

And I wonder as I hear her
that the spirit still shines through
and she can reach across the ocean deep
and break my heart in two

Mary's wise as she is foolish
she's as constant as the tide
for it's a woman's heart that beats beneath
that stubborn Irish pride
We are saints and we are sinners
We are heroes we are thieves
We are all of us beginners
on the road to Galilee

I was so flattered when I heard the song and its lyrics. It was an honour to be immortalized by such a great songwriter. She got the colour of my eyes wrong, but I guess you have to allow for poetic licence!

I invited Janis to do a duet with me on my last album, *Stories From The Steeples*. She was so gracious in accepting the invitation and so generous with her time and talent. It was such a privilege to have her on the album.

'Ladies and gentlemen, would you give your warmest of warm welcomes please to Ms Mary Black.' The crowd erupts at his words. I smile and thank Pat Kenny as I take his place on stage. I am standing in front of the Bank of Ireland on College Green in Dublin, facing an audience 100,000 strong. To my left is Bill Shanley; it is one of his first performances with me, and to my right are Frank and Pat at the ready. I shout a *Thank you!* to the audience before Pat starts into the introduction of 'Song For Ireland' on the piano. Once they hear the melody the crowd go silent and the Irish and American flags, which were shaking and swinging around in excitement only moments before, slow to a gentle sway.

> *Walking all the day*
> *Near tall towers falcons build their nests.*
> *Silver winged they fly,*
> *They know the call of freedom in their breasts . . .*

As I reach the second verse I can hear the cheers of the crowds in the distance as the cavalcade passes them. It is the first of December 1995 and President Bill Clinton is visiting Ireland for the first time.

Later that day I had the pleasure of meeting President Clinton and I could see what Monica Lewinsky saw in him! When you meet him face to face he has a powerful charisma that draws you in. As is evident from the expression on my face in the photo taken of our meeting, I gazed at him like a teenage girl meeting some American pop star. He invited me back to the White

House the following year to sing on St Patrick's Day alongside Mary Chapin Carpenter, which was a great honour.

I had become friendly with Mary after I met her backstage in Dublin following one of her concerts. She was from Washington DC and remembered coming to see me in the Birchmere when I was in De Dannan back in the early 1980s. I loved her music and I was delighted to do that duet with her in the White House.

There were a lot of Irish and Irish-Americans invited to the White House that Paddy's Day, including our president at the time, Mary Robinson. The security was very tight, as was usual at the White House, but I think it was even tighter at that time as there was still trouble in Northern Ireland. Everyone was given their own identity card before they went in, and fingerprints were taken.

It was a very grand affair, with most women wearing full-length evening gowns. After the dinner and the performance, Joe and I lined up to meet the President and his wife, Hillary. I looked around and who was queueing nearby? Only Paul Newman and his lovely wife Joanne Woodward. My knees nearly buckled when I saw him, as I loved him as an actor and always thought he was incredibly handsome.

It was such a special night; I even got a sneak peek of the Oval Office, which turned out to be much smaller than I'd imagined.

*   *   *

My tours of America were becoming an annual occurrence by this time in my life. I always tried to stick to my 'three-week rule' on those trips – which meant being away from the kids no longer than three weeks at a time – even if it meant returning home for a couple of days and going back for another stint. The tours would often stretch from the East to the West Coast, and sometimes we'd go up into Canada. It was great on those long trips to have such a fantastic group of people around me.

My relationships with the crew were just as strong as my friendships with the band, and on our nights off Damian would always book a nice restaurant for all of us. Everyone really looked forward to these days off; Maeve and I would have a lazy start, a leisurely brunch and maybe mosey round the shops in the afternoon.

The band would often slag me when we'd arrive at the airport to head out on tour as my first question to Damian was always, 'When's our first day off?' After three or four concerts on the trot and all the travelling, which was really tiring, a day off was always something I relished.

During one night off in San Francisco, I remember we all met in the lobby at seven for drinks before heading out to dinner. Damian had booked a seafood restaurant nearby, much to the disappointment of Pat Armstrong, who hated fish.

I first met Pat back in the 1970s when I was frequenting the folk clubs around Dublin. He was a lovely guitar player and played in a band called The Summertons. He had also played guitar on my *Collected* album and with The Black Family. Over the years he had become a good friend and took on the job of merchandising for my tours. Pat was over six feet tall and heavy-set; he had a big bushy beard and shoulder-length curly hair – a bear of a man who was always up for a laugh. But he was fussy when it came to his food and there was lots of food he just wouldn't touch – fish being one of them.

'Fish's eyes!' was his response when he heard where we were eating. 'You go ahead, I'll do my own thing and meet you for a drink later.'

We were used to this response from Pat when it came to where we were eating, so we headed off to dinner without him.

When we came back to the hotel for a nightcap we could see Pat was well sozzled. Apparently, on his way to find a place to eat he stumbled upon a bar that boasted, *All the beer you can drink for $10!* I'm sure that bar didn't expect a big Irishman with a thirst like Pat's to take them up on their offer. And they definitely didn't make any money out of our Pat that night! While we were enjoying our dinner, Pat was drinking beer by the jug-load and having a whale of a time.

Eventually Pat left the bar and headed off to get

something to eat across the road at the late-night diner. By this time he was starving and lorried into a big plate of burger and chips. When he went up to pay he tried to pull a ten-dollar bill out of his pocket and ripped the corner off it in the process.

In his flat Dublin accent he asked, 'Have ye a bit of sellotape there to put that back together?'

The waitress was having none of it and answered sharply, 'I'm sorry, sir, I can't accept that.'

Pat looked at her bewildered, and said, 'But there's nothing wrong with it. Sure, you just need a bit of sellotape!'

The waitress reiterated angrily, 'I'm sorry, sir, I can't accept that!'

Pat's stubbornness kicked in at this point. He put both parts of the bill on the counter and said, 'Well, that's all I have,' and walked out.

As he made his way back to the hotel with a full belly and a feed of pints, three cop cars with sirens blaring pulled into the kerb and blocked his path. Six cops jumped out and before he knew it he was up against the wall being frisked.

'Sir, did you leave that diner without paying for your meal?' they asked.

'I did not,' Pat slurred. 'I left a tenner!'

They marched him back to the diner where he had to fork out another ten dollars, untorn this time.

They let him go with a warning but needless to say there was great laughter and a lot of ribbing when we heard the story the next morning. Another night off in the life of Mary Black's band.

22

And your heart calling out to me . . .

DAVE EARLY WAS the comedian of the band; he always wanted to make people laugh. He would even make the crowd laugh during his drum solos at gigs, changing each rhythm with a pinch of humour that the crowd couldn't resist, before blasting into the end of a powerful drum solo. Backstage he would have us all in stitches recounting stories of his experiences with various different bands or jokes about him being addicted to chocolate. When he joined the band he had an amazing portfolio of people he had played with, like Sade, Chris Rea and Van Morrison.

One story he told us was about being in Van's band. At some point he had started up a relationship with Van's daughter, who was about nineteen at the time. Dave would have been in his mid-twenties so they were keeping it a secret because they knew Van would not approve. Somehow, while on tour, Van got wind of it anyhow.

One morning after a gig there was a knock on Dave's

hotel-room door. He dragged himself out of bed to answer it and Van was standing there, staring at him angrily. There were words and a kerfuffle of sorts and, to make a long story short, Dave was fired. That was the last Dave saw of Van until he joined my band.

I had met Van Morrison a few times on the scene over the years. I had sung with him on the albums *The Chieftains and Van Morrison* and *Irish Heartbeat*, and at gigs. And contrary to rumours in the industry that he was hard to deal with, I always found him to be an absolute gentleman. Any time I met him he was always very interested in me and seemed to know a lot about The Black Family and what they were up to. He would ask after my brothers in San Francisco and seemed genuinely interested in their work.

The summer of 1994 we played the Fleadh, a big festival in London. Bob Dylan and Van Morrison were headlining. Backstage there was a big space where all the trailer dressing rooms looked out on to a circular grassy area.

Dave was a bit nervous because he knew Van was there and didn't want a repeat of their last encounter. He spent most of the day keeping a low profile in the trailer. I was standing in the doorway chatting to someone outside when I noticed Van standing under a tree having a chat and a cup of tea with Bob Dylan. I whispered to Dave sitting in the trailer, 'Dave, Van's outside, don't come out here.' All I heard in response was a faint, 'Shit.' They were standing chatting for a while when Van looked up and saw me and proceeded to walk over towards our trailer.

'Dave. He's coming over. He's walking over here right now.' I knew Van knew Dave was in my band now and I was convinced he was walking over looking for him.

We were wrong. Van had just come over to say hello.

He said, 'Hi, Mary,' and we chit-chatted about the gig and what time I was going on and all that. I was tickled by the idea of Van walking away from a conversation with Bob Dylan to come over and chat to *me*. Later that day I watched from the side of the stage as Dylan, with his hood up, and Van sang together live for the first time. Dave, who was always a big fan, even managed to pluck up the courage to escape from the trailer and watch the show too.

Dave was always trick-acting backstage, telling stories and jokes and anecdotes. He always had something funny going on at every gig and made us all laugh a lot. He never drank alcohol but he did have a liking for the odd joint and was totally addicted to chocolate. He particularly loved those seashell-shaped Belgian chocolates. He would have a stash as high as my knee hoarded away at the start of each tour, but they would be devoured by the end of it.

Around 1995 we finished a long tour of the UK in Glasgow. It was a great tour; two nights at the Royal Albert Hall, Birmingham Symphony Hall and Liverpool Symphony Hall. Things were going really well for me, especially in the UK, and this was the largest set-up of band and crew we'd ever brought on tour. We even had our own catering van travelling with us.

This gave Dave a bright idea. He decided he'd go in and bake a very special cake for the end-of-tour party. It was brought out after the gig and he insisted we all have some. In fairness to him, he did tell us he'd put a 'little' bit of weed in it.

I never really liked dope; I'd had one or two bad experiences when I was younger. I just didn't like the way it made me feel paranoid and anxious. However, Dave kept insisting we all have a try, so I took a bite. It was a delicious cake, a sponge cake, really well made, and you couldn't taste anything strange about it. 'Mmm, it tastes lovely!' I said.

Dave was right on me then. 'Ah, sure have another bite, there's not that much in it.' I wasn't convinced, but as I've said, I really didn't think it tasted strong so, against my better judgement, I took another large bite. I felt OK . . . until we got back to the hotel to drop off our bags and instruments.

We convened in reception as we usually did after a gig. Everyone was debating about where we should go for the end-of-tour party and once we had decided, we then had to work out how we'd get there and how long we'd have to sort ourselves out in our rooms before heading off for the night.

Through all the hustle and bustle, the debate and indecision, in the corner of my eye I noticed three girls all dressed in black and staring at us from the other side of reception. The second I looked their way I felt a shiver from the top of my head all the way down to my toes. I can't explain why, but I instantly took a dislike and felt fearful of them.

Within ten minutes we were all barrelling into taxis to head off to some pub we had decided on. I felt strange in the taxi and when we got to the pub I tucked myself away in a corner not wanting to talk to anyone. The pub was rammed and there was a great buzz. All the band and crew were in great form at the prospect of the last night ahead. But I was a different story. It was very unlike me – I would normally throw myself into an end-of-tour party.

Joe was with me and I kept saying to him, 'I feel weird . . . I feel weird . . . I feel weird.' After a few minutes in the bar Billy Robinson, my soundman, came over to me and, pointing across the pub, said, 'Mary, I've three friends over there from Donegal. They were at the concert and they're big fans. Will you come down and say hello to them?'

I didn't know who he was talking about and was a bit uncomfortable about leaving my spot. I also didn't want to go down into the crowd. About half an hour later Billy came back to me. 'Come on down and meet them, Mary, they're really nice.' He took me by the hand and led me through the throng of people in the pub. When we got to the back of the pub, who was waiting to meet me but the three girls in black I saw in reception!

The fear started to rise in me again. Billy was busy introducing us but I couldn't hear what he was saying. My eyes were locked on their smiling faces and their hands, which were held out to grasp mine. I reluctantly shook hands and tried to smile back but all I really wanted to do was get away from them as quickly as possible and return to the safety of my little corner with Joe. They chatted away to me about how great the concert was and were all smiles and compliments. Billy joined in the conversation but I couldn't really concentrate on what they were saying because I was so freaked by them.

I think all I managed was a small 'Thanks' while trying to mask the terror behind my eyes. After what seemed like an hour of being in their presence, though in reality it was probably less than five minutes, I walked back to the corner of the pub with my face white as a ghost's. I sat down beside Joe and before he could even ask me what was wrong I blurted out, 'I just shook hands with the Devil!' Joe tried to convince me that I was being paranoid, that they were just friends of Billy's from Donegal, but my mind couldn't be swayed. In my head the three girls were the embodiment of pure evil and for some reason I was the only one who could see past their fake façade.

I spent the rest of the night in my corner not talking to anyone. I must have looked miserable, or mad – or both!

The next morning I had come to my senses. I realized that Joe was right; I was totally paranoid the whole night. We laughed about it, but it was the last time I ever went near dope. It was also the last time I believed Dave Early when he told me something wasn't strong!

It was not too long after that night that Declan left the band. Though in the beginning the prospect of not having Declan around was daunting for me, after a few months I had become confident in my own ability to move forward without him.

By early 1996 Bill Shanley had settled in well with the band and, as a whole, the band was working well together. It was around this time that I started to think about my next album and what direction I wanted to go in. I knew it would have to be in a new direction, something completely different from *Circus*. I felt my music was becoming a bit predictable and I wanted to shake things up a bit.

One evening in October that year Joe and I went to see Shawn Colvin play in Columbia Mills. I had met her a few times at festivals that summer and I had got to know her a little, though I was a fan of her music before that. She had a stunning voice and wrote her own songs. Her cover of 'Every Little Thing She Does Is Magic' brought her to an even wider audience. When I met her that summer she invited me along to her show in Dublin.

She was brilliant that night but during the whole gig it was her bass player, Larry Klein, who caught my eye. It was the way he played that held my attention; he seemed to choose unusual notes and he didn't crowd Shawn when he played but complemented her melodies and rhythms perfectly. I knew of Larry Klein before then, of course. Being a huge fan of Joni Mitchell I had seen his name on her albums and I also knew they had been married for a number of years.

After the show I went backstage to meet Shawn and congratulate her on her performance. Later that night Larry came and sat beside me. He was aware of my music and was very complimentary of my work. He gave me his contact details and told me that if ever I needed a producer he would love to work with me. This seemed like the answer to what I was looking for – the fresh start I wanted to make. I was searching for someone who would bring something new to the table, someone different to produce my next album, and here in front of me was a man whose work I highly admired and appreciated, and he was offering up his services. I could not wait to start.

Joe and Larry hammered out a deal and we started the process of recording an album. We talked to and fro about material. I had just discovered David Gray, who was gaining a following in Ireland at the time, and I wanted to record some of his songs, especially one called 'Shine'. Larry loved his songs too and sent me other material he knew, as well as some of his own songs that I loved. Larry wanted me to record in the famous Capitol Studios in LA. My idea for recording an album that was completely different was coming to fruition. I had a new producer for the first time in fourteen years, new material from writers I had never worked with before and I was recording outside of Ireland for the first time in my career.

However, during all this great excitement Larry told me he also wanted to bring his own musicians in for the recording and not use my band. Immediately, I had a problem with this. I had a loyalty to the lads, who were more than just session musicians. One night on the phone to Larry in LA I told him, 'I really want to use my own musicians. They're more than just a backing band; they're part of the sound that is Mary Black.' Reluctantly, he agreed, except for one thing. He insisted on having the great Jerry Morotta on drums and wouldn't budge on the issue. This upset me greatly; I loved Dave's playing and I loved Dave as a person. I knew it would break my heart to have to tell him he couldn't be on the album.

And I was right; it was one of the hardest calls I have ever had to make, but I was left with no choice but to give Dave the bad news. I tried to explain to him that Larry was insisting on working with Jerry; as drums and bass they came as a pair and Larry wouldn't work without him. Dave didn't say much but I could tell he was taking it badly. I talked about the work we would have when I got back to promote the album and how I would need him on the tours, but still he was quiet on the other end of the phone. I felt horrible when I put the phone down. Little did I know it would be the last time I ever spoke to Dave.

The excitement of this new venture really kicked in when Pat, Bill, Frank, Paddy Prendergast and myself arrived at the house we were staying in, which was in the Hollywood Hills. It had five bedrooms, its own swimming pool, a games room with a full-sized snooker table and a bar, and there was a beautiful view from the deck where we could see the Hollywood sign. We felt like we had really arrived at the big time.

We recorded the album in Capitol Studios in LA, and I have to admit I was in awe when I walked into the place. Iconic artists like Nat King Cole, Paul McCartney and The Beach Boys had given life to its rooms and as I walked down its long hallway that first day I saw their faces among so many others that had recorded there over the years – all staring down at me from pictures along the walls.

When I first walked into the vocal booth to do a take on a beautiful Neiman U47 microphone Larry casually told me, 'Frank Sinatra recorded on this microphone.'

'Oh really? They are beautiful microphones, I've recorded on one before,' I responded. Larry stared at me, smiling.

'No, not this *type* of microphone, this *exact* microphone.'

That didn't help my nerves, but we got started straight away. Jerry and Larry put down the bass and drums first. Then we'd go in and do our parts. Larry really brought out the best in all of us. We ended up recording five David Gray songs, a couple of which he hadn't even finished the lyrics for when we were recording. We found ourselves calling him during recording; we'd tell him we'd be doing a vocal take soon and we'd ask him how he was getting on with the lyrics. An hour later he would fax over the finished words and I'd go straight into the vocal booth and put them down.

We were in LA for five weeks. I had such a great time recording. Every day brought something different; I played with different musicians who Larry knew and explored new ideas. Everything felt good and fresh and exciting.

To cap it all, I got a little bit of a taste for the LA lifestyle; I had rented an open-top black sports car and loved driving myself around the Hollywood hills. The whole experience was a great adventure for me, personally and professionally.

Towards the end of the five weeks I was woken by the phone ringing in the middle of the night. I immediately shot up to answer it, thoughts of something being wrong with the kids flashing through my mind. It was Paddy Prendergast. 'Mary, it's Paddy. Dave has been in a car crash. He's gone.' For a few seconds I couldn't take in what he was saying and then it hit me.

I started crying and told Paddy, 'Get me a flight home in the morning.' I cried all the way back to Ireland. That was when the guilt about not bringing Dave out with us to record first started.

There was an amazing turnout of friends and musicians at the funeral: Van Morrison, Sade and so many others he had played with over the years. I sang a Sandy Denny song called 'Moments':

> *If I had my life to live again*
> *I would choose to be with you my friend*

Time moves slowly and it goes so fast
And who knows how long the days will last

My heart was broken for Dave's family and his girl-friend Mary. I had introduced them eighteen months previously and they were just about to get engaged.

After the funeral I went back to LA in a haze to mix the album with Larry, although my head was in a bad place over Dave.

One evening I got a call from Róisín, who had just turned eight. My kids were always very brave; they never put me under pressure to come home or made me feel bad that I was away. But on this night for whatever reason Róisín was upset on the phone. She was crying and said, 'Please, Mam, will you come home? I really miss you.'

None of the kids had ever asked me to come home before and I couldn't handle hearing Róisín saying that to me. I went to see Larry in the studio the next day and told him, 'Sorry, but I have to go home; my kids need me.' Larry was cool about it. He totally understood and told me to go. I trusted Larry and I was confident he could finish the mixing without me. I knew I'd be happy with the result and I flew home that evening.

Though I went home for the kids I think a part of me went home for me too. At times like that you just have to be with your family.

I was so happy to be home but still very upset about Dave. It really made me think about how precious life is and how quickly it can slip away. All these thoughts spinning around my head only made me want to be with my family more. I just needed to be close to the people I loved and who loved me.

Over the next few weeks I tortured myself with thoughts of Dave. With the album finished I had a little time off to spend at home but this only meant there was less to distract me from my guilt. I couldn't help but think that if Dave had been in LA recording the album he wouldn't have had the accident. I should have insisted that he be there. Perhaps if I'd tried a bit harder I could have persuaded Larry somehow. Maybe Dave was upset the day he crashed over not being on the album and his concentration was off. I kept replaying the last conversation I had with him, how it was so obvious, though he never made me feel bad about it, that he had wanted to come and was very disappointed that he wouldn't be involved.

One night a few weeks later I had a dream that somehow relieved me of my guilt. It is as clear to me now as it was then. In the dream I was walking towards Leonard's Corner on South Circular Road. I saw a figure standing at the crossroads about fifty yards ahead of me. As soon as I realized it was Dave he turned around and smiled at me. I immediately smiled back, I was so happy to see him. He looked absolutely shocked when I smiled back at him. When I came close to him he said with eyes wide and smiling, 'Can you see me? Can you see me!'

'Yeah, Dave, I can see you,' I replied, surprised. This seemed to make him all the more delighted.

He beamed at me and through watery eyes he said, 'I just can't believe you can see me. Please tell Mary that I'm OK and she's not to be worrying about me.' My last memory of him was his big smile and then I woke up.

I desperately wanted to fall back asleep so I could see him again but of course I couldn't, but from the second I woke up I felt a weight lift from my shoulders. The dream was so vivid, so real to me. Dave seemed so happy and well to me that after the dream I could feel my guilt slip away.

The following day I called Mary. I asked if I could see her and we arranged to meet at her flat in Rathgar. Mary was a lovely girl from Galway, a teacher, and she was desperately in love with Dave. The last time I'd seen her was at the funeral and on the day I was worried how she felt about me. Did she blame me the way I blamed myself? If she did, she never let on. She greeted me very warmly at the door and brought me inside. I could tell, though she was trying to seem happy to see me, that Dave's death had left her feeling alone and empty. He was her future, they were going to get engaged, settle down and maybe have kids one day. But now that future was gone.

I told her what had happened in the dream, that Dave was very insistent that she be told he was OK, that she wasn't to worry about him. She was happy to hear what I told her and seemed to find some solace in my words. Obviously it didn't take away the pain of losing Dave. Nothing could have done that.

23

Spirits in the wind and the memories in the stones

IN EARLY 1998 we were asked to perform in Hyde Park in London as guests for Michael Flatley's *Feet of Flames*. First created for Flatley's last show as the *Lord of the Dance*, it was a one-off performance on 25 July 1998, playing to approximately 25,000 people.

We really wanted to do it but we had already committed to a big open-air festival called City In The Park in Nottingham the same day. Damian and Joe started to look at the times we were needed at each venue. Was there a way of doing the gig in Nottingham *and* Hyde Park? The answer was yes, but it would be a tight squeeze.

We managed to get our slot in Nottingham changed to an earlier time so that we could make the Hyde Park gig. The only way to get there quick enough, though, was by helicopter. It was a hot summer's day that July and we finished our set in Nottingham at about three o'clock. If we had any chance of making it to Hyde Park in time we knew we had to grab our stuff and dash to the helipad behind the backstage area the minute we came off stage. With so many of us travelling we needed a really big helicopter, and to our surprise the one we rented turned out to have belonged to Dodi Al Fayed. It was extremely luxurious inside, with wide, white leather armchairs and drinks waiting for us on board. The pilot flew out over the crowd and as he turned all the festival goers who had been listening to us ten minutes before waved and cheered as we flew over them. It was the only time in my career I ever felt like a real rock star!

The nearest helipad to Hyde Park was in Battersea, where two limos were waiting to take us to the gig. There was an amazing buzz when we arrived. Because the weather was so good the crowd had arrived early and there was a real summer party atmosphere about the place. We had just enough time for a quick sound check and then it was all systems go.

Trevor, our backline roadie, by coincidence looked very like Michael Flatley, with short curly reddish-blond hair and the same physique. This was something that we had ribbed Trevor about for years and being the messer that he was, he took it in the best way possible. At our sound checks he would often don a black headband, roll up his sleeves tight around his muscles and burst across the stage, his tight-fisted arm held out in front of him in a hilarious Michael Flatley impersonation. All this was great fun, but now we found ourselves opening the show for the great Michael Flatley himself, and the giddy crew, headed by Minnie, couldn't help but dare Trevor to do his now famous impersonation of the great man that day.

Unbeknownst to me, while the crew was setting up, Trevor took the dare. He pushed up his sleeves, donned his ever-ready black headband and to the backdrop of *Feet of Flames* performed his best Michael Flatley impersonation ever. There was a rumble from the crowd as Trevor pranced before them and uproarious laughter from our crew at the side of the stage. However, Michael Flatley's entourage were highly unimpressed by the performance. Trevor was removed from the stage by a couple of heavies and Damian was sent for. All the crew was warned that there was to be no more messing or we would be put out.

Oblivious to all this, we went on and played a great set to a huge crowd. Afterwards I was introduced to Michael backstage and we shook hands and had a chat. He said he enjoyed the set and invited me and the band to the after-show party. The show was a massive success. As was Michael Flatley's way, his performance was a grandiose affair with flames and fireworks and beautiful girls in short dresses; the crowd went crazy for him.

The after-show party, which was just as elaborate as the show had been, was in the main hall of the Natural

History Museum. The stone steps that we climbed to the entrance were flanked by nude painted women who were posing as statues among billowing artificial flames. As we entered the hall we saw that the centrepiece of the room was a champagne bar. Inside there were more naked women posing and chandeliers everywhere. Against the walls stood stalls of food from any country you could think of: Japanese, Mexican, Chinese, French, Spanish, Italian, Thai, etc., etc. There was a giant ice sculpture of a horse with glasses around it. When you put your glass to the foot of the horse the glass would fill with ice-cold vodka. It was the most decadent thing I had ever seen and we were all loving it.

Just when I thought I'd seen it all, a fanfare struck up. The lights dimmed and a spotlight pointed towards the entrance of the room. Out of the darkness came a white stallion with Michael Flatley sitting nobly on its back . . . an *actual* white stallion! It's an image I'll never forget. What a day.

At home it was back to normal except there was a lot of excitement because Joe's godson Gavin was due to arrive from Canada.

Gavin's parents, Mick and Mags, had been close friends of ours since we met them back in 1976. Mags worked for Joe's mother Maura when Joe and I started going out. She was from Belfast and even though she was ten years older than us we loved hanging out with her, and Mick. Mick was a real Dub and told great stories; he'd have everyone around him in stitches. The two of them had this aura of kindness about them too, a warmth that you felt and connected with the second you met them.

Mick and Mags had been married for ten years when we met them and although they had been trying all that time, they were unable to have a baby. One day they heard that a priest, Father Allessio, who had worked closely with Padre Pio all his life, was coming to Dublin to give a talk at the National Stadium. With him he was bringing Padre Pio's glove, which was said to be stained with the blood of his hands from his stigmata.

Mick and Mags, who had great faith in Padre Pio, went to hear the talk that night, along with two thousand other people. After the priest finished his talk he welcomed people up to the front for a blessing. Mags got in line with her special intention in mind and when she got to the top of the queue the priest placed the glove on her head and she felt burning from her head right through her whole body. From that moment, Mags believed she would get pregnant – and she wasn't disappointed.

Ten months later Gavin Pio Leane was born. Two years after that, when my son Conor was born, we asked Mick to be his godfather. Conor and Gavin grew up together like cousins those first few years and they were very close.

But when Gavin was eight, Mick and Mags decided to emigrate to Canada where they thought they could make a better life for themselves. Mags had a sister near Toronto so she wasn't completely without family. But, like so many people who move halfway across the world, it proved to be a hard time for them and the people they left behind. We all really missed them. Gavin visited us most summers and Conor and Eoghan travelled to Canada to visit him too.

When Gavin finished high school he decided he wanted to move back and live in Ireland. He'd always loved Ireland and I don't think he ever felt that Canada was his real home. So Gavin moved into our house in Harold's Cross when he was eighteen. It was heartbreaking for Mick and Mags to see their only child leave them, and with property prices through the roof in Ireland it looked unlikely that they'd ever be able to afford to move back home.

But I think they were glad that Gavin was happy and, of course, they were reassured that we would always look out for him in Ireland.

He's an amazing person, Gavin. He inherited the best traits of both his parents, and radiates a warmth and a kindness that just reels you in and makes you feel special. He's also a very creative person and is a gifted photographer and artist, though he has spent most of his adult life caring for people with mental and physical disabilities. His beautiful daughter Aoibhe was born last year and he asked Róisín to be her godmother. I really feel Gavin has become a brother to my kids and an adopted son to Joe and me.

Another very close friend of mine who also emigrated in the 1980s was Barbara Kennedy from Ballyfermot in Dublin. I had met Barbara when I started playing basketball for Guinness's after I left school in 1974. I always loved the game and played all the way through school. Although I was short for a basketball player I had a great left-hand drive, which was unusual for most point guards, and I was quite fast too. I remember that first day walking into Guinness's club. I was just eighteen and didn't know anyone, and Barbara straight away took me under her wing. Out of that grew a very strong friendship that has lasted to this day.

In March 1979 the team went to Cincinnati to play a game out there. Friends of Barbara's organized it. It was more of a fun trip rather than a serious basketball trip. In fact, it was a great adventure, and we even got to march in the St Patrick's Day parade. After we left, Barbara stayed on a few extra days with her friends.

On her last night, she was in the local Irish pub and got chatting to a guy called Ed Kenny. He was very taken by her and asked her if she would go out to dinner with him. She told him, 'I can't. I'm going home tomorrow.' They exchanged phone numbers, he asked about her flight home and they said their goodbyes. When she got on the flight home, who was sitting in the seat next to her but Ed Kenny! He worked in aviation and was not only able to find out her seat information but that she was due to have a three-hour stopover in New York. When she sat down next to him he said, 'If I can't take you to dinner in Cincinnati, I'll have to take you to dinner in New York.' Quite naturally, Barbara was flattered and impressed and they had a great first date over dinner before Barbara left for Dublin.

Many letters and phone calls followed and I think you can genuinely say Barbara fell in love over the phone. Ed came to Ireland for a week that summer and he asked Barbara to marry him. They were wed the following December, after only meeting twice.

Following their wedding, they decided to live in the States. Moving so far away was difficult for Barbara as she didn't know that many people and she really missed home. But eventually she settled down and went on to have two baby girls, Erin and Kerry, and a few years later Eamon came along.

Through the years the two of us always kept in touch and in February 1997, when I was launching the *Shine* album in New Orleans, I invited Barbara down to spend some time with me. She booked a flight straight away but a few days before she was due to fly she called me to say she was having very bad back pain and couldn't make it. In truth, it was Ed who wasn't at all well and Barbara didn't feel she could leave him.

A few days later when I was on my way back to Ireland for Danny's confirmation I had a stopover in New York for some promotional work. I was in bed when the phone rang. It was Joe; he told me that Ed had died. He had taken his own life with a shotgun.

I immediately rang Barbara, who was inconsolable. She kept saying over and over, 'How could he leave the kids?'

I rearranged my flights so that I could be there for Barbara. In fact, I was able to sing at Ed's funeral and still make it back in time for Danny's confirmation.

Things were very tough for Barbara and the kids after that, both emotionally and financially. But Barbara found the strength from somewhere and she did a great job in rearing three beautiful kids and putting them all through college.

There have been more hard times for Barbara since then. The bank took her house and she had to move back to Ireland; she survived cancer; her daughter Erin lost her leg in a tragic accident – a whole range of challenging, life-altering experiences that would seriously test the toughest person. But throughout it all, Barbara never complained. She's always had this great spirit and energy about her and in fact, whenever I ask her how she is, she answers, 'If I was any better I'd have to sit on my hands to stop them from clapping!' She seems always to be smiling, too, and is the life and soul of the party. She's the strongest woman I know, and I have great admiration and love for her.

So many of my family and friends have emigrated over the years: Barbara, Mick and Mags, Michael, Shay, Ciaran O'Farrell, Olive and too many others to mention, but the bonds remain strong between us, which is the way it is with real friends. It's funny, when I look around at the friends that I have, a large majority of them are from the early years of my life. They know who I am and where I come from and it's those old relationships that have stood the test of time.

It was the spring of 1999 and I had been actively working on material for the next studio album, which was to be recorded later that year. I was sitting at home with Joe and the kids one evening when Joe's phone rang. It was guitarist Steve Cooney. He told Joe that he was in town and while in the train station he had seen a big poster saying *Meet Joe Black*. It was an advertisement for the new Brad Pitt movie that had been released earlier that year. However, Steve had never heard of the film and took it as a sign to call Joe.

I knew Steve through his playing with Stockton's Wing, and later through his work with Seamus Begley. I would have met him at sessions on my numerous trips to the Dingle Peninsula. He was a remarkable guitar player born in Australia of Irish ancestry. Before he came to Ireland he travelled into the outback and eventually was accepted into an Aboriginal community and became part of their tribe. In 1981 he bought a one-way ticket to Ireland, to explore his father's homeland and its music. He took with him the values and teachings of the Aboriginal people.

Steve told Joe he had written some songs he wanted to play for me, so Joe invited him over. Within twenty minutes he was at our doorstep. Six foot tall and with a big bushy black beard, Steve was a sight to behold. His impressive dreadlocks reached to the bottom of his back and were decorated here and there with colourful beads and threads. He wore a hemp woven jumper with colourful designs on it, baggy pants, leather sandals and a floppy Rastafarian-style hat.

Even though he had a big presence, he had a gentle way about him and was quite softly spoken. He also had a way with people, was always interested in what others had to say and made you feel at ease with his smile and his piercing blue eyes. I often think that animals and children can judge people in a way that adults never quite manage to do. They see past someone's image and feed off their aura, whether that be their body language or demeanour. Róisín took to Steve immediately. I thought perhaps at age nine she might be intimidated by his unfamiliar appearance, but within minutes they were talking like old friends and she was enchanted by him.

The same went for our dog Charlie, a big furry black and white border collie. Though he was always a friendly dog I had never seen him react the way he did to Steve. When Steve walked through the door Charlie went berserk, crying in happiness and jumping all over him and licking him like it was his long-lost owner coming home. Steve was as charmed by Róisín and Charlie as they were by him and he played with both of them for a long time before he got down to any singing.

After a while we settled down and Steve started into a song called 'Bless The Road'. It was a beautifully written song about lost love. I knew the story behind it already. Steve had been going out with a girl for a few years and they were planning on getting married. Four weeks before the wedding she broke off the engagement. Steve was heartbroken.

By coincidence I had met Steve and his girlfriend the previous summer on the pier at Coumeenole near Dingle. We were coming back from a trip to the Blasket Islands and Steve and his girlfriend were going out. We spoke briefly and I thought he looked unhappy that day. Little did I know she had just told him it was over.

Steve had lain low the months following the break-up and this was the first time I had seen him since. He was in a much happier mood, if a little high at times. He was excited by the stream of songs he had just written and he sang every one of them with great feeling.

If I'd experienced what Steve had been through and wrote a song about it, I definitely would not have had the generosity of spirit to compose such a hauntingly beautiful song as 'Bless The Road'. My song would have been a 'Fuck you, ye bastard. It's your loss!' kind of effort. I'll let Steve's words speak for themselves:

Remember when we walked on hills of heather,
Singing weaving mystical rings,
Now in a while my precious child,
You will unfurl your wings,
And I'll have lost what I believed
Had promised everything,
But before you go my friend my kind companion,
Listen to this song I sing.

Then go in peace and grow in grace and goodness,
Know that you have nothing to fear,
And dry your eyes my little one,
And let there be no fear.
Send me a dream from way beyond,
I promise I shall hear.

Oh beautiful, beloved, soul companion,
Thank you for those beautiful years.

And heaven hold and watch your way forever,
May your every dream come true.
Forgive all wrong always be strong,
And do what you must do.
You stand before this open door,
And you must now go through.
My special friend, my own, my sweet companion,
Bless the road that carries you.

'Bless The Road', along with another song Steve played for me that night called 'Message of Love', were to be on my next album, *Speaking With The Angel*. For this album I decided to enlist Donal Lunny to produce four of the tracks. I had worked and toured with Donal over the years and loved his production skills and playing.

The four tracks Donal produced, 'Turning Away', 'Bless The Road', 'Moments' and 'Don't Say Okay', were recorded quickly in Windmill Lane. He knew exactly what he wanted and I really liked what he did with them. I co-produced four tracks with Steve; in contrast the atmosphere in Pulse Studios was completely different, but equally enjoyable.

During this time Steve was at a very creative point of

his life. He was constantly writing and was very spiritually connected with his Aboriginal heritage; during our recordings he channelled inspiration from the Aboriginal spirit world called Tjukurrpa, meaning 'The Dreamtime'.

It's hard to describe what went on in the studio, and people often laugh and find the stories hard to believe. However, being there and watching Steve and the inspiration he drew from these spiritual beings was a fascinating experience to say the least. You'd have to see it to believe it.

Steve would at times channel the spirit of Jabirungga Nunnaguy, who would enter his body, and then, having hardly ever played the double bass, Steve would be able to play beautiful double bass lines. 'Message of Love', a song written and produced by Steve, had no fewer than fourteen musicians on the track; he used a range of instruments, including the didjeridu, harp, and even the sound of dancing feet. On the album sleeve he has credited the spirit Ngurrudu.

My good friend and soundman for years Billy Robinson engineered the album. Billy had sandy-coloured, shoulder-length curly hair and a thick Donegal accent; he was always ready with a story of the characters and the goings on in his quirky hometown of Ramelton. Billy also had an amazing pair of ears that became a very important aspect of the Mary Black sound. He's been with me now for the last twenty-five years and is a loyal and true friend whom I value greatly.

Billy was great with Steve and wasn't in the least bit fazed by Steve's unique approach to recording. Steve would often take a long time to get ready to record, banishing the bad spirits from the studio and enticing the good spirits in. He also banned all digital watches as these might cause interference too. We laughed a lot during that recording. Steve was on such good form it was contagious, as was his enthusiasm for the project.

Looking back, every album that I have recorded has brought with it its own unique story. And each one has represented a time along my journey through music, like stepping-stones across a river. Now I feel like I'm almost at the other side of that river.

All the great musicians I've worked with along the way have helped shape this journey of mine, adding their creativity and emotion to each work. So too have the producers, who brought out the best in me and the musicians I worked with.

All these people influenced me greatly, and taking a dispassionate view of each album I've recorded offers me a unique glimpse into how my life was evolving at any given time. As I developed and changed as a person, so, too, did my music and my approach to it. What was going on in my life at the time would be reflected in the albums. The ups and downs, the doubts and insecurities, the highs and lows, are all there represented in the music. I'm grateful for every album I have recorded, for each experience has taught me something, moved me forward, and the people I have worked with have helped me to become the person I am today.

24

And through the valley and over mountains, I will not forget but remember you still

WE ARE SITTING on a bench outside a rented holiday home, known locally as the Round House, overlooking the Atlantic Ocean as the sun dips down over the sea. This is the Dingle Peninsula. The sky is lit with yellows, reds, pinks and purples and the sun itself is a glowing ball of orange set low in the sky. I can still feel its warmth on my skin as I sit cross-legged, a glass of white wine in hand. The weather has been beautiful this past week, a luxury the locals keep telling us we are very lucky to have experienced because even during the height of summer the region is often bathed in mist and rain.

I sit in a comfortable silence beside my good friend Róisin Knox as we both take in the breathtaking view before us. I got to know Róisin when I started going out with Joe and when she was still Róisin Martin. She married Joe's best friend Sean Knox three weeks after Joe and I were married. Since then the four of us have grown extremely close. Her daughter Kate was born a few months after Conor, and Kate's first birthday was one of the first birthday parties Conor attended. Her first son Graham was born exactly ten days after Danny was born. The two of them first met when Graham was a day old and I brought Danny to visit him and Róisin in hospital. Danny and Graham have been great friends ever since. Róisin's second son, Jack, was born three years after our daughter Róisín, but the age gap never seemed to bother our youngest children and they always loved hanging out together as they grew up.

As the sun touches the horizon the sea explodes in a path of oranges and blues leading to the shore. As if reading my mind Róisin says, 'Is this not heaven on earth?'

It had been a magical week, our first holiday together in Kerry. Through Seamus Begley, who lived nearby, we were introduced to some of the locals and had great sessions in the local pubs, An Cúinne and An Bóthar, with fantastic traditional music and set dancing.

By the end of that holiday we had already decided we would come back the following year, and, in fact, the seed had been planted that week that would grow into more long-term plans: we thought about how amazing it would be to have our own places here.

It was a dream at first but the following summer we

started looking at plots of land big enough to build two houses set beside each other. In the end we found a beautiful field in Baile Breac near An Bóthar at the foot of Mount Brandon with a view of the Atlantic Ocean in the distance, and set about building the houses.

The houses were finished in 1999 and we spent a lot of our free time there and soon got to know the area and the way of life.

Though I grew up around singing and music, as my career progressed I found myself involved less and less in live sessions where people would gather together and play music purely for the love and the fun of it. I found this again in Kerry. I didn't realize how much I actually missed it until I was in the midst of it again. Locals like John Tommy taught me how to set dance. Séamus and his brother Brendán would play tunes and sing with friends like Lawrence Courtney and Daithí O'Sé.

We were welcomed with open arms by our neighbours, people like Dónal, Séan and Cathy Moriarty, Paddy the Yank, Tomáisín, Cáitín and Mici, and Muiris and Aileen in An Bóthar.

It's hard to describe the way of life down there and what it means to me. Being so close to Irish culture and Irish music in a place so beautifully untouched by the modern world was a great way to live.

After recording and touring *Speaking With The Angel*, I made a conscious decision to make more time for this life and spend less time on my career. My kids were growing up fast before my eyes; by 2000 Conor was eighteen, Danny was fifteen and Róisín was nearly twelve, and I wanted to spend more time with them before I blinked and they had all left the nest.

We spent amazing holidays in Baile Breac; most summers we would invite different family members and friends to join us and the kids would bring down friends who grew to love the place too.

Mammy would come down regularly every summer, too, but by that time her health had started to fail. She had arthritis in her knees; she'd also had a hip replacement, but she began to have trouble with her other hip and the doctors considered her to be too old to have another operation.

The summer she turned eighty-six we brought her down to Dingle. At this stage she was in a wheelchair most of the time, but this gave us more freedom to bring her out and about and not worry about her getting tired. We'd wrap her up well and take her on walks to Cuas, the little harbour about a mile and a half from the house. She loved to admire the wildflowers along the side of the road and the vibrant orange-coloured montbretia set against a backdrop of deep-red fuchsia in bloom.

Mammy got forgetful in her old age but she always kept her sense of humour and was a great conversationalist. Most of all, as she got older she still loved music. There was something about the music and singing in particular which brought her to life.

One summer evening we got a call to say there was a little session on in Begley's Pub in Ballydavid. Mammy didn't have to be asked twice. We bundled her into the car with the wheelchair in the back and drove the short distance to the pub.

As I wheeled her into the pub Brendan Begley spotted us and jumped up, accordion in hand. He burst into the air of 'Teddy O'Neil', a song Mammy had sung for years and which Brendan knew was her party piece. As he danced around her on light feet, opening and closing the accordion in time to the waltz, Mammy's eyes lit up. She followed his 6-foot 4-inch frame circle around her and her face beamed as she swayed in her chair. Her hands clapped and danced in time to the music and she seemed hypnotized by it all and so happy. It's an image of her that will stay with me for ever.

As I've said, as time passed I was taking on less work and spending more time with my family, especially with Mammy, and I began to feel that maybe it was a natural decline and that, perhaps, my last recording would be the *Speaking With The Angel* album. I was happy in the knowledge that my career was winding down. I had achieved more success than I'd ever expected and now I was becoming content to enjoy my life without the pressures of work. I didn't have the hunger to go back into the studio after that last album, and if it wasn't naturally there, I wasn't going to force it.

Little did I know that this was far from the end of my story, for when I experienced great loss that desire to sing and be creative became a powerful force in me again – and it was something I couldn't ignore.

The following winter Mammy had deteriorated to the point where she needed 24-hour care. Frances and I were her main carers, with help from both our families, but Mammy was getting more confused as time went on and had to be helped in and out of her chair or bed or to the toilet. So, together with our brothers, we reluctantly made the decision to put her in a home for the elderly.

She settled reasonably well but was only in the home for eight months when she contracted a bad kidney infection from which she was unable to recover.

The night Mammy died was the twenty-fifth of October 2003. Martin, Joe and most of her grand-children had been visiting her throughout the day. Frances and I sat on either side of her bed holding her hands. Brian, Frances's husband, was there too; he was very good to my mother as she got older. Danny happened to be visiting as well and I always thought it was an amazing coincidence that he was there that night.

Mammy had never been shy to tell us all that Danny was her favourite grandchild. We thought this strange because she never admitted to having any favourite children. She was once quizzed in a radio interview as to which one of us was her favourite, and after being pressed she replied, 'My favourite is the one who needs me most at any given time!'

We talked and prayed and told her how much we loved her. It was all very calm and slowly she stopped breathing and slipped away very peacefully.

Mammy had been the centre of the whole family. She held us alltogether and, in good times and bad, we flocked to her. When I came home that night I thought, who is going to fill that role now she's gone?

Keeping a family together was often a role taken up by women, so the answer was obvious in a way – it would be Frances and me.

I couldn't sleep that night because I kept thinking about Mammy's life and what she meant to me. I was torn between two conflicting emotions: I was relieved that her death had been peaceful, that she hadn't suffered and she wasn't in pain any more, yet I felt a deep sadness that she was gone.

Lying there deep in thought, a melody started to form in my mind and words flew around my head – words that resonated with meaning and somehow captured the sorrow I was feeling. After a while I decided to write them down and I eventually fell asleep as the dawn broke.

The next day I said to Danny, 'I have these words and this melody running around in my head. I really want us to finish this song for your granny.' At this stage Danny was only eighteen but he'd already impressed me with his songwriting. We sat down together with his guitar and wrote 'Your Love':

How can I say what I feel
When I turn around you're not here
I know it's my time to lead
But the emptiness inside leaves me weak

But then in a moment
It all becomes so clear
All I ever wanted was waiting right here

So now I see
Now you've been freed
That you'll always be near
Like you were all those years
And now I breathe
The life you gave
'Cos I've learned from the best
And I've always been blessed
With Your Love

> *We gathered round for your last breath*
> *Talked with you while you slept*
> *Somehow I know you'll be all right*
> *The perfect end to a perfect life*

There was a great turnout for Mammy's funeral; she was loved by so many. Michael and Shay came home with their families from America and all her children and her grandchildren were there. At the end of the mass the five of us stood around her coffin holding hands and sang, unaccompanied, 'So Here's To You':

> *So here's to you*
> *And our time together,*
> *I will share with you,*
> *A parting glass*
> *And I'll bid adieu,*
> *With some smiles and laughter,*
> *Our time apart,*
> *Will be short and pass . . .*

Later that night we had an amazing session in Mammy's house on Wolseley Street. There was music, singing and laughter and, of course, some tears.

I'd felt so hollow and empty when Mammy passed away. It seems to me that as you go through the process of organizing the funeral of a loved one, that awful hole in your chest gets filled with all the planning that's needed to get things right on the day – and, of course, you gain strength and comfort from your siblings and other members of your family. It's only when it's all over and everyone goes back to normal life that the void returns and becomes a reality once again.

The thought of never seeing my mother again was, and still is, hard to bear. But at times like this you start to think about your own mortality and wonder if there is a place where you will meet again. I like to think there is; I feel her spirit around me still and I talk to her a lot, especially when I am worried or troubled. I get great solace from that. If I turn out to be half the woman she was, I'd be happy.

Before my mother died, when we all knew that she didn't have much time left on this earth, Shay and Michael came home to see her. The five of us took that opportunity to record another Black Family album, which included some songs we had learnt from Mammy. It was released just after Mammy died and we dedicated it to her. On the album sleeve Shay wrote a beautiful tribute to her:

In early February 2003, the five of us huddled around a loudspeaker in a recording studio in Dublin. The sound coming from the speaker was the voice of our mother, Patty Black, singing songs that were familiar; songs that had been sung to us from the time we were children. The voice was frailer than we remembered; yet it was still brimful of humour, joy and mischief.

Mammy sang when she was happy, sad, exhilarated or bereaved. In her last months, during times of confusion and when having difficulty remembering the names of her children and completing full sentences, she could recall all the verses of songs she had learned in childhood. Singing was a constant in her life, and her love of music she generously shared with everyone who came in contact with her. By singing to us, her children and grandchildren, she gave us a precious gift.

We remember you for many things, Mammy, your devotion to family, your kindness and generosity to neighbours and friends and your enthusiasm for life, but passing on to us your love of singing was precious and immeasurable. We will always treasure your gift. We dedicate this album of songs to your memory.

It was a strange and difficult time after Mammy died; a few weeks later Bill's father, Mossy Shanley, died suddenly. A week after that, Damian's father Brian McCollum died. Then, in November that year, we got the news that songwriter Noel Brazil had died of a brain haemorrhage at the age of forty-six.

All of this affected me greatly and I found myself turning to songs once again.

Throughout the years I had received letters and emails from fans saying how much my music had helped them through illness or loss or heartbreak of some sort. That your music touches people is something a musician strives for and it was always a great compliment to know that my music gave solace to some people during difficult times. Now music was helping me through my own grief. I'd thought I had come to the point of fulfilment in my career, but now I needed it more than ever.

Losing Noel at such a young age shocked me. He was such an amazing talent and after he died I found myself listening to old tapes that he had given me over the years. There were songs there that had never been heard and a little fire inside me – a little voice – was telling me that I needed to record some of them. Apart from this, I also had a great urge to record the song Danny and I had written for Mammy; I wanted it to be a tribute to her.

That creative spark returned because I wanted to sing for and about the people I'd lost; the new album I was planning to record would be as much a homage to these wonderful people as it would be a form of healing for me.

What better location to record this album than in the spiritual place that had become my second home on the Dingle Peninsula?

Over the course of a couple of months we recorded the album *Full Tide* at our leisure. With Bill, Pat, James Blennerhassett (bass) and Martin Ditcham (drums), we set about turning my house in Baile Breac into a recording studio. James joined the band when Garvan left, back around 1998 after the *Shine* tour. His playing on double bass had a beautiful tone and his vocals blended very well with the rest of the band. Martin joined *c.* 2000 when I was moving back in the direction of a folkier acoustic sound and needed a drummer/percussionist who was sensitive to this style of music. Martin fitted the bill perfectly and was a lovely, gentle man. Both have become dear friends.

Billy brought down some equipment from Donegal and did a great job as engineer and co-producer. I have to say, it was the most enjoyable of all my albums to record. Being in such a beautiful place and having no time pressures made it feel more like a holiday than work. If it was a nice day we would stop for a few hours and go to the beach or go for a walk.

The musical understanding I had with the lads made the process very easy; the music just flowed out of us.

Full Tide was released in 2005. It was the first album we released on our 3ú Records label. At that stage in their lives it made sense for Joe and Paul to split up the Dara Records Company, and so Joe and I formed the third label, 3ú (meaning 'third'), which Joe ran. Joe and Paul had created Dara as the second generation after their father J.P. and now we created 3ú with the third generation in mind.

At this time Danny's band, The Coronas, were gaining momentum on the Dublin music scene and we had it in the back of our minds to record their first album on 3ú. My position in the company was more of an advisory one; it was Joe who created the platform for The Coronas that has helped them get to the level they are at today. And although *Full Tide* didn't reach the heights that some of my earlier albums had achieved, I gained great strength from it, more so than any other album I've recorded. It renewed my passion for singing and performing and made me realize that that fire hadn't gone out.

25

More than words can express, more than wealth or success

WHEN I WAS younger and my career was beginning to take off, I remember thinking, I wonder if I will still be singing at forty? Here I am at fifty-nine, and I'm still at it.

In the past few years I've been surprised at the amount of younger people coming to my gigs, particularly women, who grew up listening to me as kids through their parents, and who have now rediscovered my music for themselves. It's great to see this boost of interest from the younger generation, but it is the people who supported me in the beginning, and continue to support me today, who have made my career possible. The loyal fans that keep coming to my shows and buying my records are the ones responsible for my longevity in music, and for that I am truly grateful. Their enthusiasm and love of the music has kept me going. The ones I have met are people not unlike myself; they connect with me perhaps because they see their lives reflected in the sentiments of the songs I sing. Some of them I know on a first-name basis and it's always a pleasure to see their familiar faces. But there are some who are more than fans; they have become close friends.

In the spring of 2004, a few months after Mammy died, I was doing a concert in Cuenca, Spain. Hugo and Ria, a couple I'd met at gigs before, arrived at the sound check. They had driven from their home in Belgium to the gig and I was surprised to see that they had travelled so far to see me.

In Spain, people eat late, so after the gig we planned to go for something to eat and I invited Hugo and Ria along. They sat next to me at the dinner table and as wine was being poured Ria said, with her hand over her glass, 'No, not for me thanks.' I asked her if she didn't drink and she answered, 'I do, but there's a possibility I might be pregnant.'

'Oh, really, that's fantastic!' I smiled. 'Is it your first?'

'Well, hopefully,' Hugo answered. 'We've been having IVF treatment.'

Of course, I launched into a story about a friend of mine who had IVF three times and on the third attempt she had a beautiful baby girl.

Hugo looked at me very seriously and said, 'Yes, but this is our thirteenth attempt and it will be our last one.'

My jaw dropped. How sad that this couple had been

through so much and had, so far, been denied the joy of parenthood. They were so obviously desperate to have a child and there was a chance it might never happen for them. My heart went out to them.

'I don't know what religion you are,' I said, 'but I'm going to have a word with my mother tonight and ask her to help you.'

They smiled politely and said, 'We'll take all the prayers we can get.'

I went back to the hotel that night and I asked Mammy if she could intercede and help these people.

Two weeks later I got an email from Hugo telling me that Ria was pregnant and thanking me for my prayers. About a month after that I got another email saying that it was twins and that I could tell my mother to stop now! They went on to have a boy and a girl, Ciarán and Moira, and asked me to be their godmother. I went to Belgium and became godmother to two beautiful blond babies. We keep in touch and I see them every summer.

It was in the late 1990s that I first met Vonny Grabowsky, another fan and a special person who has been to nearly two hundred of my concerts. We were talking at an after-show signing when Vonny told me she first discovered my music when she was undergoing chemotherapy treatment for breast cancer. She explained how my albums had helped her through that tough time; while she was in hospital the songs gave her great comfort and lifted her spirits. She had a mastectomy and the chemo seemed to have worked, so I was thrilled for her.

But I think I really only got to know Vonny properly some years later. I was singing at a festival in west Cork in 2003, and after the show she told me she was taking the bus to Killarney the next day. I was heading to Dingle in the morning so I offered her a lift.

I'll never forget that trip across the mountains from west Cork to Killarney because during the course of our journey Vonny told me the story of her life. I keep telling her she should write a book because it's such an amazing story, all about her mother and father and siblings – spanning the early years of her life growing up in Indonesia, to moving to the Netherlands and then to Germany, where she had a difficult marriage and some shocking happenings after they split.

Vonny has travelled as far as America to see the shows and she often helps Joe with organizing the merchandise on tour. She's so much more than a fan now, she's a friend.

Another supporter and friend is Dominique, who was only thirteen when I first met her almost thirty years ago now. She is the niece of Michael's friend Jerry Laws, and she loves music. Although she is partially blind she has a great attitude to life and always puts a smile on my face when I meet her.

In more recent years I had the pleasure of meeting another fan of mine, actor and musician Steve Martin. I had read in an article, maybe ten years prior to our first meeting, that one of Steve's favourite singers was Mary Black, which, of course, I was flattered to hear.

It wasn't until 2008 that Joe got an email from John McEuen; he was producing an album with Steve Martin and said that Steve was very keen to have me sing one of the songs on it. Steve played banjo and had invited other artists like Dolly Parton, Vince Gill and Tim O'Brien to sing on the album, too.

The song they had in mind for me was a bluegrass tune called 'Calico Train'. They asked if I would fly over to New York to record but I was just back from a long trip to America and I wanted to stay close to home, so I asked if I could record it in Dublin. They agreed and we set a date for the week before Christmas in the Cauldron Studios in Dublin.

Initially we thought just the producer was coming over with the backing track, but the weekend before the recording date Joe got a call from Steve. He said he'd really like to come over for the session and asked if Joe would book a nice restaurant for afterwards.

Joe said of course, and asked him, 'What time is your return flight, Steve?'

'Around nine thirty,' Steve replied.

Alarm bells went off for Joe when he heard that.

'Well, we better get an earlier booking than seven p.m. How about five o'clock, so you have enough time to check in?'

'Ah, don't worry about that,' said Steve. 'We have our own jet.'

As well as Steve, John McEuen and another five-string banjo player had come over for the trip.

The Cauldron Studios is in a basement on Blessington Street and I was a little nervous as I came down the steps to meet Steve. As it turned out, Billy, who was engineering the session, said that Steve was quite nervous to meet me beforehand! After the initial introductions we got down to it and did the recording in a couple of hours and everyone was pleased.

We went into a restaurant in Nassau Street after the recording session and we all settled into a relaxing dinner. Steve, who had been a bit shy earlier, began to loosen up after a glass of wine, telling stories and cracking jokes.

Our American friends were all desperate to hear some Irish music, so after dinner we piled into their stretch limo and took them to the Cobblestone Pub in Smithfield. There was a session in progress, with pipers, fiddles and flute players belting out some trad tunes at the front of a packed pub.

We managed to squeeze our way in and no one seemed to notice Steve in his fedora hat and horn-rimmed specs.

The three boys were reluctant to bring their banjos into the session, so they left them in the car. Steve asked me to sing and I said that I would, but only if they brought in the banjos to play a few tunes. Surprisingly, they agreed. I belted out 'I Live Not Where I Love', unaccompanied, as Joe was dispatched to get the instruments from the driver.

A great session ensued until Steve was spotted and the word began to spread through the pub. It wasn't long before there was a queue of people lining up to have their photo taken with him. He initially obliged, but we quickly realized it was time to go and we said our goodbyes before he got mobbed.

As I've said, the fans have really been great to me over the years. In this digitally driven world they have followed my more recent endeavours online and I have got to know some of them that way, too.

With all the technology around today, it seems that the music industry has completely changed; it doesn't compare to the music world when I started out. Now everything is online and a person's career can be made by one YouTube video. It is not a career that I would advise anyone to enter into lightly and that's the advice I have given my own kids.

When the boys were younger they wanted to learn the guitar. They both loved music so, along with their cousin Eoghan, I got them lessons with Bill Shanley. Danny was only about eleven at the time, while Conor and Eoghan were fourteen and fifteen.

The older boys picked up the lessons much quicker than Danny, who became frustrated by what he considered to be his lack of progress. I never pushed my kids with music, I always wanted them to do it for themselves, but when Danny came to me saying he wanted to quit guitar lessons I argued with him about it. I told him to hold on a bit longer and to keep at it; I promised he'd never regret learning an instrument, he just had to be a little patient. Reluctantly, he kept at it and I'm pleased to say eventually something clicked and he caught up with Conor and Eoghan. He hasn't looked back since, and as he grew I encouraged him to write his own songs. 'That's where all the money is, Danny!' I would tell him. His best friend Graham took up bass and along with another friend, Conor Egan, on drums they started to play together.

They were a bit rough around the edges to begin with, of course, but they worked hard and by the time they were in college they'd improved a lot.

It was in Vancouver on their J1 summer visas that they met another guitarist, Dave McPhillips, and that's when 'The Coronas' were born.

I remember the first time I realized that they had something special. The four boys were still in college and had a sell-out gig in Whelan's. When I arrived there were queues around the corner to get in and there was pandemonium at the show. People were rammed up to the stage singing along to the songs.

The band already had this strong following after only one single, 'Decision Time', released on 3ú Records, and Joe and I were convinced then that this was the start of something big. We went on to record their first album, *Heroes Or Ghosts*.

We've now finished recording their fourth album, and The Coronas have genuinely established themselves as one of the leading bands to come out of Ireland in the last ten years, headlining venues like the O2 and the Marquee. They have recently signed to a major publishing company in the UK called Big Life Music and have just negotiated a worldwide record deal with Island Records. To say we are proud of Danny is an understatement. Apart from the music, he is a well-rounded individual who has time for everyone he meets.

From the moment she could make noise our daughter Róisín loved to sing. When she was a toddler, her godmother Anne Maloney would buy her books and Róisín would look at the pictures and sing the story to Anne instead of waiting to be read to. When she was only three or four, Janice would be singing around the house and Róisín would often tell her she was singing out of tune.

She was like my mother in that she never had to be asked twice to sing, and you could see the passion on her face when she sang.

I brought Róisín on tour with me to Japan in 1997 when she was eight; it was the first time she got up on stage to sing with me and that's probably where she got the bug. After that show I could see she was buzzing and she hasn't lost any of that enthusiasm since.

I always thought Róisín had a great voice for a child, but I remember the first time she really blew me away. The Black Family first started performing on the annual Irish Festival Cruise around 2000. Michael brought his three girls on the trip and Shay brought his youngest, Shosí, and they all did Irish dancing during our show.

I asked Róisín if she wanted to sing and she said she wanted to do Eva Cassidy's haunting version of 'Somewhere Over The Rainbow'. She was only thirteen at the time and I remember telling her that this was a very difficult song to sing and I suggested she picked something a little easier, more simple. But she was determined and even roped in the great accordion player/pianist Phil Cunningham to accompany her on piano. When it was time for her performance she stood up and sang like I'd never heard her sing before and she received a standing ovation from the audience. It was a really special moment.

When she was in her late teens, Róisín started

gigging with her cousin Eoghan, who is a great guitar player and songwriter. After recording an EP she joined me on tours abroad as the support act. It soon became obvious from the reaction of the audiences and her EP sales that it was time to record an album. The year after she left college, she recorded her first album, *The Secret Life of Blue*, with a great band of young musicians she had met along the way; it was recorded and produced by David Odlum in France. Since then she has headlined around Ireland, supported the likes of Lionel Richie in the O2 and Ryan Sheridan on his German tour, and has recently signed a record deal in Germany.

It can be difficult for Róisín being a singer and the daughter of Mary Black as well as the sister of Danny O'Reilly. However, she has developed her own unique style and is following her own musical path. I have no doubt that she's a better singer than me and I am very proud of her. I always felt blessed to have a little girl after my two boys, and my daughter has grown up to be a talented, clever, beautiful woman who has also become my best friend.

As for Conor, my first-born, he will always have a special place in my heart. From a young age he was gifted at sports and was particularly good at any sport that involved a ball. He just had a natural athletic ability and even as a two-year-old toddler he was able to kick a ball out of his hands. In school Conor excelled at tennis and basketball, but his first love was always Gaelic football.

He is a talented musician, too. He learned guitar from a young age and later taught himself to play bass. In fact, he played bass on my last album and, given that he wasn't a professional musician, our engineer was amazed at how quickly he did his takes.

But despite his musical ability, I don't think Conor ever had that drive to perform like Danny and Róisín. While he has a huge love of music, he was never really interested in being on stage. In a way, I think the football pitch was his stage. He has such a great passion for the game. At 6 feet 5 he plays midfield for our senior team in Templeogue Synge Street and I am just as proud seeing him soar through the air and catching those high balls for our club as I am when I see Danny or Róisín on stage.

Conor was the wild one of my three kids, or at least he was the one who got caught the most. The other two were too cute. By the time they were in their teens, they had learnt from Conor's mistakes and knew how to get around Joe and me. Either that, or we were too pre-occupied with Conor's antics to notice theirs!

He was always very independent, and I think it was perhaps because he wasn't the baby of the family for long and more was expected of him as the eldest.

He inherited his mathematical brain from his father and got a degree in Geomatics in college. But he wasn't one for settling down and he travelled the world several times in his twenties, exploring different countries and meeting people from different walks of life. Though he got a good job in Dublin City Council as a land surveyor when he was twenty-seven, it wasn't until his partner Jade gave birth to our beautiful granddaughter Bonnie that he became a changed man. With Bonnie's arrival it was like he had a new purpose in life and he has put his heart and soul into taking care of his family and being a good father.

He is constantly striving to make a lovely home and a good life for Bonnie and Jade, who is an amazing mother and a beautiful person. I am so proud of the way Conor has taken on the responsibilities of fatherhood with such love and enthusiasm. Needless to say, Bonnie has brought great joy to the whole family and she has also brought us all even closer together. As I write this I am staring at her beautiful little sister Fía Rose who just arrived last week; another little miracle to love.

Joe and I have been so blessed over the years. We're lucky to have had three healthy and happy kids who have grown into three well-rounded adults and now we're enjoying being grandparents too.

On top of all of this, there is Joe. From the beginning he always encouraged me and believed in me, even when I didn't believe in myself. As my husband, manager and partner in our record company, Joe has protected me from a lot of the rough side of the music industry. This can be a tough old business, and it's so important to have someone you can trust standing beside you, supporting you and helping you to make the right decisions. There are so many artists of my generation who have been ripped off and overworked by the record label executives – by managers, hangers-on and others who should have been looking out for them. That was something I never had to worry about. Joe always made sure that I was getting a fair deal and never pushed me to take on more than I could comfortably manage. Besides, he wanted me to be at home with the family as much as I did.

Since I was nineteen Joe has been my best friend. He was, and is, an amazing father to my kids, who hold him in such high regard and still look to him for guidance in adulthood. He has been a constant presence in both my personal life and my career these last thirty-five years and I couldn't imagine my life without him.

Looking back at all the stories of my life it seems I could have taken so many different paths.

I was always proud of the fan base I'd built up in the States and I remember how, at the height of my career, with every US tour the crowds grew larger.

But despite this success I often wondered what might have been if I'd accepted an offer that came my way back in 1991.

Dick Whitehouse, who was the Curb Records A&R man in Nashville, always felt that the song 'Past The Point of Rescue' could be a hit in America. He first heard it on the *No Frontiers* album before Curb signed the US deal with me. Dick thought that it would do well if it was given a country feel, and they asked me if I would do a duet with a new up-and-coming country singer called Hal Ketchum. In fact, Bill Straw called to ask if I would be interested in going over to Nashville to record with Hal.

I didn't know Hal Ketchum then and I was extremely busy with my own career at the time. I think I had just come back from a long tour and wanted to hang out with my kids rather than go back to the States and record with someone. I didn't know. In the end, Hal went ahead and recorded the song without me.

'Past The Point of Rescue' became a huge hit for Hal Ketchum worldwide. It was the most played song on American radio that year and without a doubt it made Hal a star. I was delighted for Mick Hanly, another one of Ireland's great songwriters, who benefited greatly from his song's success.

As I've said, I often wonder what direction my life would have taken if I'd taken up that offer. It could have changed a lot of things. I might have ended up living in America; I might have had huge success there on the back of the song; it could have been hugely beneficial financially, too. We will never know.

The truth is, I really don't regret passing up that opportunity. In fact, looking back, I have very few regrets about the decisions I have made.

While my success in the grand scale of things might be considered by some to be relatively small, I am still more than satisfied with the way my career has gone. I believe there are reasons why things happen or don't happen and that fate plays a part in our lives. As my mother always said, 'What's for you won't go by you', and I've lived by that mantra. I have met hugely successful female artists who have sacrificed their home life and some even sacrificed having children for the sake of their careers. Most have lived to regret it, and I knew from the outset I would never let that happen to me. My proudest achievements are my kids; they have always been my priority, and for all the success that the trip to Nashville might have brought me, I'm still glad I chose to hang out with them instead.

This is the last call

Now, in the year 2014, I find myself in the midst of my *Last Call* tour. After recording and touring *Stories From The Steeples* in 2011, I decided that my next big tour abroad would be my last.

Over the course of the six years between *Stories From The Steeples* and my previous album, *Full Tide*, a collection of songs had found their way to my ears that prompted me to go back into the studio. Many of these songs told a story, and we recorded most of them up in Billy Robinson's Steeples Studio in Ramelton, hence the title.

I have to say, *Stories From The Steeples* is one of my favourite albums from my catalogue. It has a simplicity and honesty about it and I got to sing with some great artists, such as Janis Ian, Imelda May and Finbar Furey.

Alongside Pat Crowley, Bill Shanley and Martin Ditcham I also got to record on *Steeples* with two musicians who had been in my touring band since 2008:

the internationally acclaimed saxophone player Richie Buckley from Dublin whose playing always moves me and is a great man to tell a good joke on tour, and Belfast-born Nick Scott, a brilliant bass player, who also lends beautiful vocal harmonies to the live gigs. They slotted into the line-up seamlessly, both in a creative and personal way.

The songs this time came from diverse sources – among them Shane Howard, Eric Bogle, Ricky Lynch and three new songs from my son, Danny O'Reilly. I loved Danny's quirky 'Wizard of Oz' and I always fancied covering 'Faith in Fate' (in my mind one of Danny's best songs). It's become a feature of the live gigs with Richie playing a breathtaking sax solo.

The decision to make this my last tour was made less difficult because I am not completely retiring from singing. My earliest memories are of singing and I could never imagine living my life without it in some form. I think I will still do one-off shows, festivals abroad and some gigs in Ireland when the mood takes me. But I just want to give up the gruelling side of touring – the travelling from city to city, the driving and flying here and there for weeks on end. After thirty-five years of touring I feel I've had enough and want to make time to enjoy other aspects of my life.

This is, of course, slightly tinged with sadness because I know there will be a period of adjustment, and there will be times when I will miss all the buzz and the madness that comes with being out on the road. It's been part of my life, and it's been a lot of fun in so many ways, but I feel the time is right.

I've been asked if I will ever record another album and my answer to that question is: I don't really know. If the songs call me, then maybe I will. It's always been about the songs, and I guess it always will be.

Being a Gemini (the twin sign), I've always felt that my life took two roads. So over the years I've learned to wear two hats: one is for Mary Black the singer, performer and musician; the other is for Mary Black the mother, wife and friend. I couldn't imagine being fulfilled without either side of the coin, and I've been lucky enough to have had a healthy serving of both.

I remember one afternoon when I was out washing my windows. I had just got back from London that morning after playing two nights in the Royal Albert Hall. When I walked in the front door I noticed that the windows needed cleaning.

I got straight on with the job that afternoon. I had changed into an old pair of raggy jeans and a T-shirt. I was standing on a chair in the front garden cleaning the windows when a car slowed down outside the house and a man I didn't recognize rolled down the car window and stared at me from the driver's seat.

'I don't believe it! Mary Black!' he shouted. 'I was at

the Royal Albert Hall listening to you singing last night and today you're out cleaning your windows?'

All I could do was shrug my shoulders, laugh and say, 'Ah, sure, that's my life for ya.'

Permissions

Song extracts

Prologue: 'Schooldays End' Written by Ewan MacColl. Published by Harmony Music Limited on behalf of Stormking Music Inc.; 'Another Day' (Jimmy MacCarthy), Sony Music.

Chapter 6: 'Beautiful Bundoran', traditional.

Chapter 11: 'It Was Pleasant and Delightful', traditional; 'The Leaving of Liverpool', traditional.

Chapter 13: 'The Rose of Allendale', traditional.

Chapter 15: 'The Broom of Cowdeknowes', traditional; 'Colcannon', traditional.

Chapter 16: 'No Frontiers' (Jimmy MacCarthy), Sony Music.

Chapter 17: 'Babes in the Wood' (Noel Brazil), Little Rox Music.

Chapter 21: 'Mary's Eyes' (Janis Ian), Rude Girl Publishing; 'Song for Ireland' written by Phil Colclough & June Colclough. Published by Bucks Music Group Limited on behalf of Leola Music Limited.

Chapter 22: 'Moments' (Martin Hayworth), Signalgrade Music.

Chapter 23: 'Bless the Road' (Steve Cooney), MCPS.

Chapter 24: 'Your Love' (O'Reilly/Black), Little Rox Music;

'So Here's To You' (Alan A. Bell), Tamlyn Music Ltd.

Chapter titles

Prologue: *Me, facing me* from 'Crusader' (Mick Hanly), Peer Music UK.

Chapter 1: 'Down Our Street', traditional.

Chapter 2: 'Songs of Pleasure and of Love', traditional.

Chapter 3: 'God Bless the Child' (Herzog/Holiday), Edward B. Marks Music Company.

Chapter 4: 'Schooldays Over' (Ewan MacColl), Harmony Music.

Chapter 5: *Hey Little Brother* . . . song lyric from 'Another Day' (Jimmy MacCarthy), Sony Music.

    sub-heading: *Her simple smile is Heaven's gate* . . . song lyric from 'Wonder Child' (Jimmy MacCarthy), Sony Music.

Chapter 6: *All the world shall be of one religion* from 'I Live Not Where I Love', traditional.

Chapter 7: *Oh, what you wouldn't give to be down on that pier once again* from 'Ellis Island' (Noel Brazil), Little Rox Music.

Chapter 8: *An open door was to a girl like the stars are to the sky* from 'The Moon and St Christopher' (Mary Chapin Carpenter), EMI Music.

Chapter 9: 'The Loving Time' (Noel Brazil), Little Rox Music.

Chapter 10: *I've got no more smiles to win you* from 'Circus' (Noel Brazil), Little Rox Music.

Chapter 11: 'And the Larks They Sang Melodious at the Dawning of the Day', traditional.

Chapter 12: *This child, he means the world to me, there is no more enchanted* from 'Wonder Child' (Jimmy MacCarthy), Sony Music.

Chapter 13: *When Mary left her highland home and wandered forth with me* from 'The Rose of Allendale', traditional.

Chapter 14: *And I wish I was back home in dear old Dublin* from 'Paddy's Lamentation', traditional.

Chapter 15: *Oh, weren't them the happy days* from 'Colcannon', traditional.

Chapter 16: 'No Frontiers' (Jimmy MacCarthy), Sony Music.

Chapter 17: *Remember when we walked on hills of heather* from 'Bless the Road' (Steve Cooney), MCPS/IMRO.

Chapter 18: *Great dreams and laid schemes* from 'Still Believing' (Thom Moore), Little Rox Music.

Chapter 19: *And there's peace in a travelling heart* from 'Columbus' (Noel Brazil), Little Rox Music.

Chapter 20: *Caught between the settled life and on the road again* from 'Mountains to the Sea' (Shane Howard and Neil Murray), Mushroom Music Ltd.

Chapter 21: 'Who Knows Where the Time Goes' (Sandy Denny), Fairwood Music International .

Chapter 22: *And your heart calling out to me . . .* from 'Katie' (Jimmy MacCarthy), Sony Music.

Chapter 23: *Spirits in the wind and the memories in the stones* from 'Don't Say Okay' (Shane Howard), Australian Mushroom Music/ Bob-A-Lew Songs.

Chapter 24: *And through the valley and over the mountains, I will not forget but remember you still* from 'So Here's To You' (Alan Bell), Tamlyn Music Ltd.

Chapter 25: *More than words can express, More than wealth or success* from 'Flesh and Blood' (Shane Howard), Mushroom Music.

Final chapter: *This is the last call* from 'Ellis Island' (Noel Brazil), Little Rex Music.

Acknowledgements

In 2010 I was approached by Eoin McHugh from Transworld Publishers who asked me if I would be interested in writing my autobiography. The prospect of writing a book had never occurred to me. I wondered would there be much interest in it. As well as that, I was in the midst of touring and had plans to go into the studio to record *Stories From The Steeples*. So I passed on the offer, but I think it planted a seed in my mind.

Eoin approached me again in late 2013. This time I gave it more thought. I was a little apprehensive at the prospect and sought the advice of an old friend and gifted writer, Theo Dorgan. His encouragement was invaluable to me and the one thing he stressed was that it should be written in my own voice.

At that time I had also decided that after thirty years I was ready to hang up my touring boots, and it seemed that this book could be a nice way to mark that. Theo's advice stuck with me. I knew I would need someone to help me get the stories down on paper, but I wanted that person to be someone I knew and who knew me. I asked

331

my daughter Róisín if she would type up a couple of stories for me and in October 2013 the two of us got stuck into writing. The memories and stories started to flow and Róisín began to question me about different aspects and details of the events. She had been an avid reader from a young age and seemed to have a natural understanding of the process. It was a precious time spent with Róisín. I would sit with her and tell her the stories while she listened and typed. Often when I was finished she'd rub her hands together and say, 'OK, Mam, now let's set the scene.' She always managed to ask the right questions and really gave shape to the chapters in an intuitive way.

The more stories I told as the book progressed the more I realized how much I was leaving out. There are many people who have been part of my life who haven't been mentioned in this book. That does not make them any less important to me; you know who you are. However, I hope this book gives a flavour of what my life was about and who I am.

I would like to thank Eoin McHugh and Brenda Kimber at Transworld Publishers for giving me the push and help I needed to write this book. Thanks to Róisín, my best pal and daughter, for giving shape to the project. To my family and friends, for all the love and laughter along the way. To the musicians and songwriters who lent me their talents and creativity. And finally, to the fans; without your support none of this would have been possible. Thank you for giving me the career I love so much.